T0266692

The Story of Grace by Horatius Bonar (1808–89) is aptly named as the author unfolds the beauty and mystery of God's redeeming grace in the Lord Jesus Christ and his gospel. Appealing to all who will hear—but with a heart and mind towards the young person in the church— Bonar tells the story of grace through the events in the Garden of Eden under our first parents. Thirteen chapters of meditative systematic covenant theology direct the reader time and again to give glory and praise to the one who came down and sought his own. This small book will be a go-to for encouraging young people, small groups, and meditative and devotional times of private worship. Highly recommended!

NATHAN ESHELMAN
Pastor, Orlando Reformed Presbyterian Church
Orlando, Florida

The Story
of Grace

An Exhibition of God's Love

Horatius Bonar

CHRISTIAN
HERITAGE

Scripture quotations are based on the *King James Version.*

hardback ISBN 978-1-5271-1189-9
ebook ISBN 978-1-5271-1262-9

Published in 2025
in the Christian Heritage imprint
by
Christian Focus Publications Ltd,
Geanies House, Fearn, Ross-shire
IV20 1TW, Scotland
www.christianfocus.com

Cover design by Daniel Van Straaten

The Fell Types are digitally reproduced
by Igino Marini. www.iginomarini.com

Printed and bound by Gutenberg, Malta

CONTENTS

FOREWORD

If someone asked, 'If you could choose any Scottish minister from ninteenth-century Scotland to be *your* minister, who would it be?' I would be hard-pressed for the answer. But not because of a lack of choice. To be able to listen to the oratory of Thomas Chalmers couched in his Fife accent, to hear the remarkable Thomas Guthrie, founder of the 'ragged schools' for children, to sit at the feet of the immensely learned William Cunningham or George Smeaton, to listen to the young W. C. Burns or Robert Murray McCheyne in the same week in the latter's pulpit in St Peter's, Dundee, or to sit under the ministry of the remarkable number of godly and gifted ministers God gave to the Scottish kirk in those days—it would be difficult to choose just one.

But if I had to choose one, it might just be the ninteenth-century minister whose name appeared in the credit lines of some of the hymns I learned to sing as a youngster.

He penned the beautiful communion hymn, 'Here, O my Lord, I see Thee face to face'; the anthemic 'Blessing and honour and glory and power'; the gospel-rich 'Not what these hands have done Can save this guilty soul'; the strong exhortatory 'Go, labour on; spend and be spent'; and my own favourite, based as it is partly on the words that first brought me to faith, 'I heard the voice of Jesus say'. The minister is, of course, the author of this thoughtful and beautiful book, Horatius Bonar.

Horatius Bonar (or Horace, as his friends knew him) was born on 19th December 1808 and died on 31st July 1889. He came from a long line of presbyterian ministers; two of his brothers were ministers; his best friends were ministers—including his brother Andrew, Robert McCheyne, John Milne of Perth and others who were caught up together in the evangelical awakening that blessed Scotland in the mid-nineteenth century. Horatius served an early pastoral apprenticeship in Leith and thereafter became minister of the North Church in Kelso for two decades before returning to Edinburgh as minister of the newly formed Chalmers Memorial congregation.

Bonar's life was surrounded by friendships, but it was also punctuated by sorrows: five of his nine children died within a short space of time; in later life one of his daughters was left a widow with five children and returned to the family home. He did not have his burdens to seek. But his experience of what Paul describes as 'the riches of his grace' (Eph. 1:7) and the peace and comfort, encouragement and joy which he found in Christ, suffused his ministry.

He embodied the portrait in Interpreter's House in John Bunyan's *Pilgrim's Progress,* of the minister who—

> had eyes lifted up to Heaven, the best of Books in his hand, the Law of Truth was written upon his lips, the World was behind his back; it stood as if pleading with men, and a Crown of Gold did hang over its head.

Bonar's faithful ministry, caring for his flock and seeking the lost sheep is still expressed not only in the hymns he composed but also in the books he published and in the dozens of beautiful evangelistic 'Kelso Tracts' he wrote.

In *The Story of Grace* we find the essence of Bonar. In it, he uses the opening chapters of the Bible to tell the story of the whole Bible, of Eden created and spoiled, and of how paradise is restored in Christ. He does so with a simplicity that helps us appreciate the profundity of the gospel of the grace of God. Now almost two hundred years old, it remains fresh and readable. If you know next to nothing about the Christian faith, these pages will help you. If you have been a Christian for many years, these pages will help you to recalibrate your appreciation of God's grace.

I suspect that when you are finished reading *The Story of Grace*, you will agree with me that it must have been a great blessing to have had Horace Bonar as your minister—because in these pages you will have had a real taste of his ministry for yourself. Better still, you will have experienced the central burden of that ministry—to show you grace by showing you the Lord Jesus Christ.

Sinclair B. Ferguson

Preface

I have used the expression, 'Story of Grace,' which will be found to occur, not only on the title page, but once and again throughout this volume, not so much because of its simplicity, as because it seemed to me the exactest for bringing out the real nature of the gospel, and for helping us to shake off from it the misconceptions which self-righteousness has, in so many forms, hung around it, defacing its comeliness and clouding its sunshine. God meant the gospel to be not so much a *profession* of love, as a visible *exhibition* of it; not so much a *declaration* of feeling, as a *history* of facts. His object is not only to address us in words that may be heard, but in deeds which may be seen and felt.

He knew that it is not enough for Him to *say* to us that He is gracious; the reiteration of this truth, however frequent and fervent, would not suffice. He who fashioned our natures, knew that it is not thus that hearts are won.

If He would find His way into them once more, He must *display* as well as *declare* His grace.

Mere professions of love do oft-times only harden us against its influence, closing the ear that they are meant to open; for it is so easy to use the warm language of love, even when love itself is cold. The heart may be emptiest when the voice is loudest; and we are ready enough to value but slightly that which costs nothing but words. Besides, what comes to us indirectly, and by inferences of our own, from clear facts and deeds, is more powerful than what reaches us more directly. We delight far more in gathering up the broken fragments of affection, as they silently scatter themselves along the course of some artless story, than in listening to the most fervent exclamations and asseverations of love.

Therefore, it is that He who formed our natures has taken this way of reaching and winning them. It is thus that he steals round them with gentle attractiveness, that, before we are aware, our hearts may be led captive and bound in the fetters of his love. He has embodied his love in deeds, and given us the story of what he has done and of what he means to do. He does not come up to us directly and say, 'I love you,' but he does the loving deed: he brings to pass the gracious event; and thus, there is suggested to us, with irresistible impressiveness, the thought, 'Oh, how he loves!'

It has been said of human affection, that it has no need of language to give it utterance. The look can convey the feeling better than the word, and 'eye can well interpret eye.' If, then, the look and the eye be so intensely expressive, how much more the *deed?*

Thus it is with God. He does the loving deed, and then records it in all its simplicity, without one word of colouring or comment. He does the gracious thing, and then writes down the story of it, that we may read in it the riches of His grace, and that, in thus reading, we may be blessed.

That story is the simple record of love's doings on behalf of the beloved object. In regard to these doings there can be no mistake. They do not admit of a double interpretation; they do not leave us in any doubt as to the gracious mind of the doer. They make it plain; plainer even than words or affirmations. Besides, they are more winning and more irresistible; they are facts which can have but one meaning—facts which can lead but to one conclusion, a conclusion such as that which the Apostle drew when he said, 'Hereby perceive we the love of God, *because He laid down His life for us'* (1 John 3:16).

The story of grace, then, is the story of God's doings in grace with this world of ours. If we speak of it in reference to the Father, it is the story of His thoughts and purposes from eternity. And what grace there is in these! If in reference to the Son, it is the story of His doings and sufferings upon earth. And what grace there is in these! If in reference to the Spirit, it is the story of His witness-bearing to this manifested grace of the Godhead. For He is the narrator of the wondrous tale! Thus, the loving purposes are the purposes of the Father, the loving deeds are the deeds of God the Son, and the loving testimony is the testimony of God the Holy Ghost.

The story of grace is the truest that has ever been told on earth. He who tells it is true, and He of whom it is told is the same. In it there is no intermixture of true and the false; it is absolutely and altogether true, in every jot and tittle. Only this may be said of it, that whilst it is 'a true report which we have heard' (1 Kings 10:6), yet the half has not been told us.

Nothing so wonderful has ever been wrought out of man's fancy or drawn out of human history. It is 'stranger than fiction.' Yet all is simplicity. No colouring of art is laid on for the sake of attractiveness; Scripture always taking for granted that the real can never be indebted to the unreal for interest or effect.

Nor is it more marvellous than blessed. It contains God's own proposals of friendship to us. It speaks of peace—a purchased, finished peace, through a divine peace-maker—peace between the sinner and God, between earth and heaven. It points to rest, rest for weary man. Its object is to fill us with God's own joy, to make us sharers of God's own blessedness. In listening to it we find the burden of our guilt unfastening itself from our shoulders, and the bondage of a troubled conscience giving place to the liberty of reconciliation and love.

It is a story of the *heart*. And the heart whose feelings it transcribes, whose treasures it unlocks, is the heart of God.

It is this story of grace that has brought back something like sunshine into this world of ours. For though light has not yet displaced the darkness, still it is no longer midnight. 'Through the tender mercy of our God, the dayspring from on high hath visited us, to give light to them that sit in darkness and in the shadow of death, to guide our feet into the way of peace' (Luke 1:7-8). Morning still lingers, as if struggling with prolonged twilight, or as if the sun were rising under an eclipse: but the promise of day is sure: the noon is near.

It is this story of love that has shed peace into so many souls, and unburdened so many consciences of their loads of guilt. Many a wound has it healed; many a broken heart has it upbound; many a feeble limb has it strengthened; many a care-worn brow has it unwrinkled; many a dim eye has it rekindled. It has gladdened earth's melancholy wastes with fresh fragrance and verdure, sadly reminding us of the paradise we have lost, yet brightly pledging to us the hope of the better paradise hereafter, when, under the dominion of the second Adam, the desert shall rejoice and blossom as the rose.

It is this story of love that God has been telling for these six thousand years. He calls it 'the gospel,' or the good news, or the glad tidings of great joy. And so it is. Yet how few receive it as such, or give God the credit for speaking the truth when He makes that gospel known to us! 'Who hath believed our report? And to whom is the arm of the Lord revealed?'

I have sought in this volume to open up a part of this wondrous story—that part of it which God made known to our first parents. In this fragment, we may be said to have the outline of the whole. It was told partly in Eden and partly out of it; partly before 'he drove out the man,' and partly afterwards. Both of these scenes I have endeavoured to sketch.

I have written generally for all classes and ages; but I confess I have often, throughout, found my eye turning to the youth of our day—to those who in the pride of opening manhood and womanhood are hewing out, each one his own cistern, to be broken as soon as hewn, and eagerly asking, 'who will show us any good?'

Many of these are ensnared with the fascinations of a present evil world. Its cup tastes sweet to them, and they would fain prolong the draught. The 'lust of the flesh, the lust of the eyes, and the pride of life,' are leading them far astray. Life seems to open on them like a summer's dawn. They hurry along, eager to enjoy its brightness, and impatient of every obstruction that besets their path. Perhaps the thirst of gold has already seized them, sealing up their hearts against all that is large, and loving, and holy. Or, perhaps, it is the delusion of romance that dazzles. Earth, with its tales or dreams of love; earth, with its music and mirth; earth, with its poetry and song; it is this—it is this that is seducing the soul and ensnaring the opening affections. They drink into the sentiment in which one of the poets of modern pantheism exults:—

> High swells the joyous bosom, seeming
> Too narrow for its world of love;

Nor envies in its heaven of dreaming
The heaven of gods above!

No wonder that it should be hard to win their hearts to God, or draw their ear to listen to His voice. The very name of religion seems to chill them, sometimes to irritate them.

But shall we allow them thus to waste their immortal being, to feed their famished souls upon the world's husks or the world's poison? Shall we not tell them how sadly they mistake when they fancy that there is joy only in that gay world of pleasure? There is such a thing as joy elsewhere, joy purer and sweeter than they have ever tasted. There is love deeper, truer far than that of earth. There is a tale of love to which earth's highest stretch of romance can make no approach. It is to this tale of infinite love that we would invite their ear.

It is one which runs through many ages, opening and widening as it passes along. I have tried to lay hold of it at a single point, when emerging in its brightness from the shadows, which man's sin had drawn over the earth. To trace it in its after-progress, as told by patriarchs, and prophets, and apostles, and, above all, as proclaimed by Him who was in the bosom of the Father, and who came down to tell us of the grace that is there, would far overstretch the limits of this slender volume. But the theme is too full and rich not to invite a return to it if such be the will of God.

Horatius Bonar
Kelso,
November, 1847.

I

How God Told the Story of Goodness in Eden

Among the many orbs that are moving to and fro throughout the silent heavens, there is one on which God has bestowed peculiar care, as if in connection with it he had some vast design to unfold. From the pains that he took upon its construction, and the delight he expressed at the completion of its adornment, it is plain that in it he was laying the foundation of some mighty fabric, fixing the centre of some stupendous system, preparing his plans and models for the ordering of the universe throughout the everlasting future.

That planet we call earth and speak of it as our native star. It is there that we had our birth, and it is there that we receive our better birth. It is there that we live and love; it is there that we sorrow and rejoice. It is there that we lie down in dust; and it is there that we await the sound of the resurrection-trumpet, when He who is our life shall appear.

Let us try, then, to read the history of our native planet, and listen to the story which it has been telling since it arose in beauty from the hand of God. As the dwellers upon its surface, we hear and see all things near, not afar off. We are not like men receiving imperfect tidings from some distant region; we stand in the very centre of the wondrous scene. We can search into the roots and beginnings of all that we behold; we can trace the stream, through its strange windings, backwards to its clear source in the lonely mountain glen, where the sunbeams are freshest, and the turf spreads out around us its fringe of purest green.

This earth, as it came out of the mould of the former, was altogether goodly. He who made it has told us how much He was satisfied with its beauty. It was good, very good. Nought but blessedness breathed through its atmosphere or shone in its light. It was a world in which God could entirely delight, for there was not a stain on its face to offend His holy eye.

No blight was preying upon its verdure or consuming its flowers. There was health in its sunshine, and balm in its fresh soft air. No clouds were blackening its firmament, and treasuring up the wasteful lightnings. No storms were rending its forests or ruffling the ocean that girt in its happy shores. All was comeliness and perfection. In each sight and sound there were repose and joy.

Man, too, was holy. He knew not what it was to sin, nor how such a thing as evil could find its way into a world so fair. He saw it excellent, and how it could lose its excellence, or become less perfect, he could not conceive. Paradise was for him, and he for paradise; the dweller and the dwelling suited each other completely; the outer and the inner circle of being fitting in to each other in all their parts, proportions, and motions. God, too, was with him—the maker of this wondrous earth and these infinite heavens—conversing with him, instructing him, blessing him with light and love. He had rested from His work and came down to hold fellowship with man. The seventh day's dawn brought with it peace, the very peace of God. The calm of the Sabbath was there, a Sabbath like that which angels keep in heaven, a Sabbath such as earth has never since been gladdened with, but which we know it is yet to taste when the second Adam comes to make all things new.

It was then and thus that God began to tell the story of his *goodness* upon earth. 'How great is His goodness!' was the living utterance coming forth from everything created. He had been telling that story in heaven from the time that there were any creatures to tell it to; that is, from the time that He populated heaven with the blessed angels. In what way He had been telling it there, we know not; through how many ages it had been running, no record is given. But He had a purpose to tell it elsewhere, and to other beings besides the angels. For this end He gave birth to the earth, that He might tell it there; that

He might have another circle which it should traverse in a new form, and that thus He might make known more widely how glorious in *goodness* He was.

For each happy scene on earth spoke aloud of this goodness. Each pure star above, and each rich flower below, told the story of this goodness. It was written over the whole earth in letters that all could see; it was spoken over earth in tones that all could hear. Each scene distinctly breathed it; the sounds of sweet harmony, that went and came over the face of creation, had each a voice that articulately made known the story of this goodness. 'Day unto day uttered speech, and night unto night showed knowledge' (Ps. 19:2). What a story! How full, how vast, how varied! Each hour, each moment, God was telling it to man, that man might rejoice more abundantly in Himself, and find what a portion for his soul is the favour of that Infinite Being, out of whom all this goodness was pouring itself. And each hour, each moment, man might have been singing, 'O Lord, our Lord, how excellent is thy name in all the earth! Who hast set thy glory above the heavens' (Ps. 8:1). 'Thou art worthy, O Lord, to receive glory, and honour, and power; for thou hast created all things, and for thy pleasure they are and were created' (Rev. 4:11). 'Great and marvellous are thy works, Lord God Almighty' (Rev. 15:3).

In all this it was not merely wisdom and power that God was displaying. It was *goodness*. It was His heart that God was opening up to man, for it was the knowledge of that, that alone, which could make him blessed. Man might know much of God, but if he knew not this, he could have no enjoyment. Everything depended upon his knowing that the heart of Him who made him beat lovingly towards Him. This was life, and, without it, life could not be. This was the charm of being, and, without it, existence could not but be a blank, nay, something more terrible—a curse!

It is not the works of God that can gladden us, however perfect, if separated from His heart. It is not the knowledge of His wisdom, or His greatness, or His majesty, that can fill our souls with peace. If these are disjoined from His paternal feelings, they can only amaze or terrify us. It is God himself, the Father of our spirits, that is our real portion. He only can fill us; and with His fulness set our hearts at rest. His largest gifts are nought to us without Himself. They are precious in themselves, but, apart from Him, they cannot satisfy nor bless. It is the love of the Giver, not the beauty of His gift, that meets the cravings of the human spirit. Let us clear up this a little more fully.

I look up at that blue sky which bends so brightly over me. It is without a stain. From the horizon to the zenith, it is perfect in its beauty; there is no flaw in the whole stretch of its azure circle. I cannot but admire it, and still more the mind that planned, as well as the hand that painted it. But is this all that it awakens in me? If so, then I am like one admiring the fair-written characters of a language which I have no skill to interpret. Nay, but it is not all. There is much more than this to be discovered there. That radiant arch is not only the indication of an infinite mind, but it is also the utterance of an infinite heart. It is effulgent with love; it glistens with parental smiles. I dare not separate between the beneficence of God's works and the benevolence of His heart. In the former I cannot but read the latter. These heavens most plainly tell me what is the heart of Him who made me. They show me how it beats towards me, and how it yearns over me with an intensity of affection and interest which it is impossible for me to overestimate or overprize. And it is this that makes me glad; it is this that is the warmth of my spirit, the very pulse of my being. That blue arch that encompasses me about seems like the infolding pressure of the everlasting arms. Every gleam of it sends a thrill to my heart more joyous and satisfying than does the conscious possession of the tenderest love of earth.

Or, again, I walk forth by that mountainside, where the wildflowers blossom, without a hand to sow them, and scarce an eye to see them. I take up that tuft of heath that buds as gaily as if a thousand eyes were on it. How beautiful, how perfect! But of what does it tell me? Of the wisdom of God. And is that all? No, surely. It speaks of something more than the mind of Him who clothed and coloured it so richly. Does it not speak of His *heart*? We do not merely say, as we look upon its purple clusters, 'If this be so passing beautiful, what must He be who is the fountainhead of all beauty?' We say, also: What must be the *heart* of Him who has taken such pains upon that world which He made for us, so that even its very wastes are fair and fragrant! In all that He has been doing, He seems to have been thinking of us, of our comfort, of our happiness! In every leaf, in every blossom, in every odour, in every colour, He seems to have been consulting always for us, thinking how He could make us happiest, how He could continue to pour out most of His heart upon those scenes in the midst of which He meant us to dwell.

When thus looking at His works as laying open His heart, we get at their real meaning. We understand the story which they were meant to tell—a story about the heart of God. They are God's revelation of Himself. And they are just such a revelation of His character as is fitted to bring glory to Him and joy to us.

It was this story of divine goodness, as told upon earth by God, that made man so blessed. The happiness of the creature came directly from what he knew of this loving creator. It was not Eden, but the God whom Eden spoke of, that was his joy. It was not the fair sky of an unfallen earth that made his eye glisten as he looked up into its depths; it was the God whose goodness he saw shining there so richly. Each object made him happy, by showing him God, and drawing him into fellowship with Him. Acquaintanceship with God was all he needed for his blessedness. This acquaintanceship each scene around was fitted to increase.

Nor did he find his joy in thinking of himself or contemplating his own excellencies. He did not say, 'I am a holy being, I never sinned, I always obey God; surely I am entitled to be happy.' No, his joy lay in God alone, and it was in thinking about God that this joy flowed into him. The more he knew of the Infinite One, the All, he was the happier. To forget himself and remember God was his true delight. Every new insight into the heart of God was to him an increase of gladness, a new wellspring gushing forth in paradise. God's favour was the sunshine of his being, and everything that spoke more fully of that favour glistened with that sunshine and poured new streams of life into his soul. In Eden, as in heaven, God was 'all and in all'—God Himself, the living God, the personal Jehovah, in whom man lived and moved and had his being. Perhaps it was something of this kind that the German poet meant when he thus spoke of creation:—

> With my own burning thoughts it burn'd,
> Its silence stirr'd to speech divine;
> Its lips my glowing kiss return'd,
> Its heart in beating answer'd mine.
> How fair was then the flower, the tree,
> How silver-sweet the fountain's fall!
> The soulless had a soul for me,
> My life, its own life lent to all.

Yet these words, though beautiful, do not strike the true key; at least, they contain but half the truth. It was not a certain abstract principle, called deity, that Adam saw in the scenes around him; it was the one living Jehovah, a real and a personal friend, that walked with him hand in hand through that blessed region, conversing with him face to face. This was something of which the poet knew nothing, and for which his religion makes no provision;

nay, it is something which his system wholly shuts out, as being both unpleasant and untrue. It is not the living God that he sees in everything; but he worships everything as if it were the living God!

It is no mere name that man is called on to recognise in creation, no shadow clothed with what are termed attributes or perfections; it is the very life of the universe, the Being of Beings, the eternal I AM. He it is with whom man met in Paradise, and of whom all things spoke so blessedly.

Reader, and especially *young* reader—for this scene of Eden-brightness seems to speak home to the young and opening heart—let me deal with you for a moment. Is this Infinite Being *your* God? Is his favour your life, his smile your treasure, his friendship your all? Is it in Himself that you have found your joy? Are you using His works for the purpose of making you happier in Him; or are you perverting them to the awful end of making you happy *without* Him? Do they bring Him into you, or do they shut Him out? Are they prized for the discoveries which they afford you of Him, or because they help to fill up the void within, and make you no longer dependent upon Him for happiness? He built those mountains, up whose slopes your young elastic step delights to climb. He poured the clear water into those streams on whose banks you love to wander. He made that glad day, with its bright sun, and that solemn night, with its ever-sparkling gems. What, then, must *He* be who did all this for you? What a portion must His favour be? What endless gladness must be in

His smile! What a heaven upon earth must be enjoyed in fellowship with Him! This was enough for your first father, when unfallen; it may well be enough for you! He whose name is Jehovah is the one Being whose friendship would be infinite gain to you, and the loss of whose acquaintanceship would, of itself, be a hell as terrible as the region of the unquenchable fire.

2

How Man Interrupted
This Story

This scene of gladness was not abiding. Man broke in upon it, as if already weary of it, before it had well been tasted. He interrupted God in telling the story of His goodness upon the earth. He sinned. The story ceased, and the voice of goodness forthwith died away.

This interruption by man was strange indeed. It seemed impossible that a being thus blessed should ever have ceased to listen to his God, that he should so soon grow weary of God, and of that blessedness which he had so plentifully found in Him. It would not have been strange that God should be tired of telling this story of His goodness to man; but it was truly strange that man should so soon have become tired of listening to that story from the lips of God. Yet so it was at the first, and so it has been found ever since that day. God has never said to man, 'I am weary of thee, depart from me!' but how often has man said to God, 'I am weary of thee, I desire not the knowledge of thy ways!' He was not weary of Eden, perhaps, but he was weary of that God who met him everywhere, and whose voice seemed to come forth to him from every leaf and flower.

Immediately he showed this. He stretched up his hand and plucked from the forbidden tree the fruit of which God had said, 'Thou shalt not eat of it.' What did this mean? That he had become weary of God and had begun to prefer the gift to the Giver, and that, for the sake of the gift, he was willing to lose the favour of the Giver.

In denying him that fruit, God meant him no harm; He did him no wrong; but He put him to an open test—a test for the will and the heart. He said, 'By this let me see whether thou carest most for the Giver or the gift, which of the two is the more precious in thine eyes.' For a while the Giver was everything—the gift was nought when compared to Him. But the choice soon began to alter; the eye admired the fruit; the heart coveted it. God seemed to stand between man and the desire of his heart. That heart immediately whispered, 'Where is this goodness now? Is He not a hard master?' Unbelief overcame; he laid hold of the tree; its fruit had become his God; he saw more to be desired in it than in God; he closed his ear against the story of God's goodness; nay, he denied the whole truth of that story. The very meaning of his disobedient act was, that this goodness was but a profession, this whole story of it a lie! He gave the lie to God; he gave the lie to the many voices that whispered around him of that goodness—he gave the lie to all Eden, with its holy beauty. He said, 'God is not good, whatever these flowers may say; God is not good, whatever these stars may utter; God is a hard master, for He has denied me this fruit, which my heart desires.' Thus he believed the devil; he gave reception to the serpent's calumny; he took the suggestion of his own heart; he turned away from God; he preferred the gift to the Giver; he cast out the Creator, and put a small fragment of his handiwork in his place, saying to it, 'Be thou my God!'

Thus, man interrupted God in telling the story of His goodness. He would hear it no more; he little thought how much remained untold, what stores of blessedness might have been opened to him as the story went on. He turned away from God and from His voice, as if he had heard enough.

But God would not be mocked. It was a true story that he had been telling to man, and He could not suffer His word to be discredited, and His goodness denied, by the creatures He had made. Besides, He was holy, and could not but hate this hideous sin; He could not treat it lightly, as if it did not concern Him. He must now speak in another voice such as man had never yet heard—a voice which would let man know how He hated that which he had done.

And this voice of holy displeasure must, like the former, come forth from all the works of His hands. They had all been telling of His goodness; they must now begin to tell of his righteousness. Each object must have an utterance; each part of creation must proclaim in man's ears, regarding this holy God, 'Thou art of purer eyes than to behold evil, and canst not look upon iniquity' (Hab. 1:13); 'The wages of sin is death' (Rom. 6:23); 'Cursed is every one that continueth not in all things that are written in the book of the law, to do them' (Gal. 3:10). That same world that had been telling so universally of His goodness was now to tell as widely that there was something more than goodness in God; that there was such a thing as righteousness; nay, that 'He loved righteousness and hated wickedness.' Sin was now to 'reign unto death,' in order that God might thereby express his abhorrence of evil: that is to say, death was to be shown to be the certain issue of everything in the shape of sin. This was the brand with which God was to stamp creation, to make man fully know that sin was 'the abominable thing which he hated.'

Nor did this take long to accomplish. It took effect without delay. God but withdrew His hand from the instrument out of which the rich music had come forth, and straightway its chords were unstrung, and from each one there came forth the sounds of discord and sadness.

The skies began to darken, as if to hide the face of God, and to show that this was no longer a world fit for God to look upon. The storm came forth in its fierceness, as if to let man hear how an angry God can speak, and how terrible is 'the thunder of his power' (Job 26:14). The verdure faded, the leaf grew sere, the weed sprang up, the flower drooped, the creatures looked fiercely on each other, hoarse sounds went and came, and the harmony of earth was dissolved. The world seemed to be putting on sackcloth, as if bewailing some unspeakable calamity that had smitten it. It stood now like one of those mourners of whom history speaks, whose fresh locks a single night's grief has blanched, whose clear forehead has been made, by some overwhelming stroke, to take on at once the deep wrinkles of age.

It was thus seen that God was angry; and that, in each one of these sad changes, He was giving awful utterance to His displeasure against man for the sin that he had done, for the disobedience of which he had been guilty. He would now feel what a 'fearful thing it was to fall into the hands of the living God' (Heb. 10:31).

That curse is still upon the world. God did not withdraw it after a brief season. It is a long as well as a heavy curse; and this poor, dying world—this world of graves and darkness—proclaims that infinite curse as loudly as it did at first. There are no signs of abatement, no tokens of any lessening of God's fierce anger against *sin*; nay, it cannot abate, it cannot be quenched. It is *eternal*. And why? 'For the righteous Lord loveth righteousness' (Ps. 11:7).

Son of Adam, that curse is upon you, if not yet a son of God! The sin that is in you God hates. He cannot trifle with it, as you are doing. If He makes as light of it as you do, what means this heavy, unabated curse? What mean the groans of creation? What means this life of sorrow, this heritage of tears? What mean the pangs of disease, the tossing of the sick bed, the unsated hunger of the grave?

What mean our broken ties and our bitter farewells? Are these things known in heaven? Do these blightings fall upon worlds into which sin has never found its way? Or, when angels visit the earth, do *they* become the heirs of grief and death? No, for sin is not found upon them. But these evils are *your* dark lot—a lot which you cannot flee from—for *you* have sinned! The accursed thing cleaves to you; and however lightly you may estimate it, you have but to look around you on the suffering earth, or within you, to be taught that God's estimate is very different from yours. Every withered leaf you tread upon, every cloud that passes over you, every pain that tears your body, every grief that casts its shadow on your soul—all tell you how God cannot tolerate sin in any form, however lightly you may treat it, or however harmless you may deem it.

The evil of sin is infinite; God's hatred of it is unchangeable; and woe be to that creature, were he the highest angel, on whose skirts one single stain of it is found!*

---

* 'Oh, sin—sin is just hell!' was the bitter cry of an awakened spirit. Another, who for two years had groaned under unhealed convictions, was asked whether he had yet thoroughly seen the evil of his own heart. His reply was, 'I have—I have seen to the very bottom of hell.' Andrew Fuller: English Baptist minister and theologian (1754-1815) thus narrates his convictions:

> The reproaches of a guilty conscience seemed like the gnawing worm of hell. I do not write in the language of exaggeration. I now know that the sense which I then had of the evil of sin and the wrath of God was very far short of the truth; but yet it seemed more than I was able to sustain. In reflecting upon my broken vows, I saw that there was no truth in me.

I saw that God would be perfectly just in sending me to hell, and that to hell I must go, unless I were saved of mere grace, and, as it were, in spite of myself. I felt that if God were to forgive me all my past sins, I should again destroy my soul, and that in less than a day's time. I never before knew what it was to feel myself an odious, lost sinner, standing in need of both pardon and purification. I knew not what to do! In this state of mind, as I was moving slowly on, I thought of the resolution of Job, 'Though He slay me, yet will I trust in him.' I paused and repeated the words over and over. Each repetition seemed to kindle a ray of hope, mixed with a determination, if I might, to cast my perishing soul upon the Lord Jesus Christ for salvation, to be both pardoned and purified; for I felt that I needed the one as much as the other. In this way I continued above an hour, weeping and supplicating mercy for the Saviour's sake (my soul hath it still in remembrance, and is humbled in me); and as the eye of the mind was more and more fixed upon him, my guilt and fears were gradually and insensibly removed, I now found rest for my troubled soul.

3

How God Overruled Man's Interruption

There were many reasons for not executing speedy sentence upon man, and upon the world which he had ruined. No careful reader of the scriptures should be at much loss to discover these. They are written all over the Word of Truth.

God had His own reasons for allowing sin to enter. These same reasons inclined Him not immediately to arrest its course. These reasons will open out as we pass along. Meanwhile, at the very outset, let us suggest a few.

He wished to show us what sin is.
An evil, an infinite evil; so great an evil, that He must not bury it out of sight, nor sweep it away, till He has made the whole universe look upon it and see its loathsomeness. He let it run its course, now that the floodgates have been

opened, in order that it may show itself fully and spread itself out in all its hideous variety, exhibiting itself, not in one form, but in ten thousand times ten thousand forms.* *He* knew what sin was and what was in sin. But *we* did not; nay, we could not. We must see it in detail. It must be spread out. He knew what that one small seed contained; but we could not, unless we saw the whole of this 'boundless upas, this all-blasting tree.' Therefore, that seed is allowed to take root and spring up, and ripen its fruit, and spread its branches over all the earth. Thus, God meant to show us 'the exceeding sinfulness of sin,' to teach us that it is not merely a calamity over which He grieves, but an evil which He utterly hates, and against which His wrath must be directed in all its fierceness.

He wished to show the wickedness of the creature.
It is not one sin that he will commit, but millions. It is not in one thing that he will prefer the gift to the Giver, but in everything. It is not in one particular that he will mistrust or deny the Creator's goodness, but in every particular, great and small. Nay, he will hate God. He will mock God. He will defy God. He will become an atheist altogether.

---

*   Thus one wrote eighteen years ago: 'That sin should poison life's fountain in a being created so noble as Adam; that sin should poison the streams of life in all their branches; that one sin should engender from its venomous drop enough of suffering to steep a world in misery—is indeed an awful truth.... one of the mightiest demonstrations of sin's iron grip and deadly hold, proving it to be all but the mightiest power in being.' Most truly and not too strongly spoken!

God did nothing to make man wicked or to deprave his heart. No, He merely brought up to the surface the abominations which that heart contained. Nor was this the state of one heart alone. It was that of millions. It was that of each child of this fallen father.

He wished to show the union between sin and sin.

Sin is not an isolated thing, which, as soon as it is done, disappears without a trace or scar. It is necessarily, and by its very nature, linked with a thousand others. Cast a small pebble into the broad ocean, and it raises a ripple which expands, circle after circle, and ceases not till it has rolled itself upon the most distant shore. So with sin—with one single sin—even what we call the slightest. It is the root of millions. It perpetuates itself forever. Like the ocean ripple, its influence is beyond all calculation. Yet there is this difference between them. The ripple grows fainter and sinks lower as its circle widens and recedes from the centre. Not so with sin. What was a ripple at first, soon swells into a wave, ever rising higher, till we behold the huge, dark mountain billow breaking upon the eternal shore.*

---

* This law which regulates the spiritual world is the very same as that which on the lower scale of being regulates the natural world. A distinguished man of science in our day has given us a chapter in one of his works, 'On the Permanent Impression of our Words and Actions on the Globe which we Inhabit.' Its conclusions are startling, and, viewed in connection with the laws of higher being, most solemnising. 'The principle,' writes he,

He wished to show the creature's helplessness.

He can sin, but he cannot undo the effects of sin. He can unfasten the link that binds earth to heaven, but he cannot reknit it. He can cast himself out of heaven, but he cannot raise himself up to that lost heaven again. It is not needful that God should consume him or bind him in chains of darkness, that he may be prevented from re-entering God's presence. It is enough that he be left to himself. His utter helplessness becomes sufficiently manifest of itself. Deliverance must be of God if he is to be delivered at all. His creation was of God, and it is to be seen that his new creation is also of Him, and of Him alone. God made him

---

of the equality of action and reaction, when traced through all its consequences, opens views which will appear to many persons most unexpected. The pulsations of air, once set in motion by the human voice, cease not to exist with the sounds to which they give rise. The motions they have impressed on the particles of one portion of our atmosphere, are communicated to constantly increasing numbers. The air is one vast library, on whose pages are forever written all that man has said or woman whispered. But if the air we breathe is the never failing historian of the sentiments we have uttered, earth, air, and ocean are the eternal witnesses of the acts we have done.... No motion impressed by natural causes or by human agency *is ever obliterated*. The momentary waves raised by the passing breeze, apparently born but to die on the spot which saw their birth, leave behind them an endless progeny, which reviving with diminished energy in other seas, visiting a thousand shores, reflected from each other, and perhaps again partially concentrated, will pursue their ceaseless course till ocean itself be annihilated (Babbage: *Bridgewater Treatise*, pp. 108-114).

at first, and that was much; and He is to re-make him out of sin, and that is more.

He wished to open up his whole character, as the infinite Jehovah.

This was his opportunity. Now He could fully bring out to view all that was in His mind and heart. He could not be seen as the healer till some were sick. He could not be known as the helper till there were some to succour. He could not be known as the renewer of the world unless it were seen how far that world could go into decay. Therefore it was His purpose, neither to arrest sin at once, so that it might not be committed again, nor to destroy that earth where sin had arisen, that no trace of pollution might remain; but to suffer it to prolong its existence, and thus afford the occasion of His unfolding the fulness of his infinite mind and heart.

He wished to make creation more immovable.

By man's sin and by the sin of the angels it had been proved how unsteadfast the creature was. If a third race had been created instead of man, there would just have been another fall. God had shown how frail the creature is, even in the most favourable circumstances. Therefore, God proceeds no further in creation till He has laid a far deeper foundation for it to rest upon. This He goes on to do. By the incarnation of His Son, He links creation to Himself in ties that cannot be broken.

O, the depth of the riches both of the wisdom and the knowledge of God! How unsearchable are His judgments, and His ways past finding out!
(Rom. 11:33)

Perhaps, reader, you are one of those who in this age are setting their hearts on knowledge. It is well. But here is knowledge, the deepest and the fullest of all. You are aspiring after science—longing to scale its heights. Here is the first of science—science truly divine. The knowledge of creation, in all its parts and proportions, and substances and laws, is counted science, and eagerly sought after. Nor is it an unworthy knowledge, nor one which an immortal spirit might not delight in. But if the *laws* of the universe be worthy of your studious inquiry, what must the great framer of these laws be? If the worthy composition of this earth and its substances be meet for your most earnest search, what must He be who created and arranged them all? If the motions of the heavenly orbs be so wonderful, what must the great mover be? Have you studied Him? It is an infinite study; and oh! What a recompense of joy does it bring along with it! What marvels and what mysteries does it disclose! To know the wonders of earth is good; to know the wonders of heaven is better and nobler still; but to know Him who made, and who fills both earth and heaven, is more blessed, more excellent, more glorious, by far.

4

God's Purpose
Unfolding Itself

It was the story of His goodness that God had hitherto been telling. It was this that man had interrupted; and by so doing had exchanged life for death, becoming heir to the threatened curse of God, and subject to His immediate wrath. What, after this, could be looked for, but the departure of God from earth, and the entire cessation of His goodness towards man?

But God had another purpose—deeper and more marvellous than this. It now came up into view.

God's full character had never yet been known. Its breadth and length had never been brought to light. It was but a small portion of God that had hitherto been revealed. He had, indeed, displayed as much of Himself as could be done in a world where all is sinless. But this was not enough. It needed a new state of things to bring out the rest. This new state God did not introduce, for no sin takes origin with Him. But man introduced it. He committed the trespass, and so altered the condition of the world as well as his own. It was in connection with this state of evil that God's purpose now began to develop itself.

A state of evil does not seem to man the likeliest for unfolding the heart of God. A world where all is light without any darkness, union without any jar, holiness without any sin, appears to us the likeliest world for calling forth into manifestation the whole fulness of the divine nature. There love would be met with no coldness, no rude challenge of its sincerity, but with the full response of sympathy from every eye and heart. Fellowship would be unbroken, joy would be unmingled, and in this flowing and reflowing between heaven and earth there would be a continual increase of all that is good and blessed. Were this to go on eternally, surely there would be room enough, and occasion enough, for God to bring forth His largest treasures?

So we might reason. But we forget ourselves when thus attempting to sketch plans for God. A perfect world like that would certainly answer the question, does God love those that are like Himself? But it would not solve the far deeper and more difficult problem, has He love for those that are *unlike* Himself? He loves the loving and the loveable; can He love the unloving and the unlovable? He can *punish* sin, as was seen in the angels that left their first estate; but can He *pardon* it? He can banish the sinner from his presence; but can He receive him back again?

And if there be such forgiving love in Him, how far will it go? Will it embrace only a few of the best and the least unlovable, or even the worst, even the chief of sinners? And if so, is it love that is ready to make sacrifices for the beloved object, to grudge no cost, however vast, in order to compass its designs? These are questions which can only be answered in a fallen world, and among a race of sinners. A perfect world can give us no information respecting them; not so much as one slender hint. It is utterly silent; for its experience only ranges within a certain limit. It testifies only of the holy, and of their mutual fellowship and joy.

Yet it is the solution of these problems, the answer to these questions, that can alone bring out the depths of the divine character. One half, at least, of that character must otherwise have been concealed. One half of love's true nature, and that the deeper and the more marvellous, would have remained unknown. Its upper surface would have shone in eternal loveliness, but its depths could never have been sounded; its unfathomable mines of gold and silver would never have been explored; its treasures would never have been imagined. The outer chambers of the heart would have been open and accessible, but its inner chambers, its deep and infinite recesses, would have been unseen and unentered.

Has it not been so even with the natural world, over which the fall has drawn its melancholy shadow? Has not that dark event been the means of opening up the resources of the earth and heavens, of drawing out of them new objects for our admiring gaze? It has spread over us the cloud, but in it, it has given us the rainbow. It has seared the verdure of the earth, but it has given us the matchless tints of autumn's yellow leaf. It has raised the winds, but it hath brought the white foam of the billow from the transparent blue beneath; it has called up, in all its vastness, the storm's 'magnificently stern array.'

And has it not been thus also with man's heart? Have not strange discoveries been made in it, as if new strings had been added to the harp, carrying its notes far deeper on the one side, and far higher on the other?

When is it that the mother's heart comes out in all its fulness? Not in prosperous days of health, when her face beams gladness over each member of the happy circle. It is in the hour of sorrow, when one of her budding roses has been early blighted, and death seems about to rob her of the joy of her heart. Look at that sick bed over which she bends with such intensity of sadness. Till now she did not herself know what love was in her. Each wan smile of the dying countenance, each contortion of the features, each wistful upturning of the bright eye, seem to open up new fountains of love. But look again. The disease seems passing off. Health is regaining its dominion in that dying one. What a revulsion of joy—joy which can only get vent to itself by unlocking another region of her heart and letting forth new streams of love upon the recovering child. In the one case, what depth of sorrowing love, and in the other, what heights of rejoicing love, were opened up! The human heart is discovered to be a thing of far wider compass and capacities than could otherwise have been conceived. It is by means of the objects and scenes of a fallen world that this discovery has been made. They introduce us into new regions of being and of feeling such as could not have been entered on through any other avenue or made visible from any other point of observation.

Just so has it been with God, and such is the method He has taken for making known to us this same discovery with regard to Himself. Nothing but a world of sin and suffering could have afforded such an opportunity. And it is here, accordingly, that God is opening up the full extent of His love. I do not thus speak of the fall as if it were an *unexpected* event, and as if God were merely taking advantage of an unforeseen occurrence in order to forward His own ends. Far be this from Jehovah, the God only wise, whose plans are all from eternity. Yet we may thus speak after the manner of men, as He Himself has taught us to do: ever remembering, however, that redemption is no mere expedient to remedy a sudden and unlooked-for evil, but the very design of God, whereby from everlasting He meant to glorify Himself by the full revelation of His whole character to the universe which He had made.

A world unfallen reveals but half of God. The deep recesses of His character only come out in connection with a world fallen. The heights and depths of His infinite nature were not manifested, till that which is opposed to them occurred to bring them forth. To learn what holiness is, and how holy God is, we need not merely to see His feelings towards the holy but towards the unholy. In order to discover the extent of His goodness, we must not merely see its connection with what it loves but with what it hates. In the sinless world we see how the loving meets with the loving, the blessed with the blessed; but we have still to learn how the loving meets with the unloving, how the blessed meets with the accursed. Does the heart of God yearn over the lost? Does it pity the suffering and the sorrowful? Has it pleasure in the death of the sinner, or, would it rather that he should return and live? Does it remain uncooled by the sinner's coldness? Does it, when grieved, still suffer long? Does it, when rejection thrusts it away, and hatred opposes it, still cast its eye of unextinguished tenderness towards the poor outcast that refuses to be blessed? God's dealings with a fallen world were the full answer to all these questions. And what an answer!

Thus God overruled man's interruption of His story of goodness. We shall see more specially how He did so in the next chapter. Meanwhile, it is blessed to notice how very different were the results flowing from the introduction of sin, from what we could have imagined. God's thoughts are not as our thoughts, nor His ways as our ways (Isa. 55:8). He purposed not to arrest or annihilate the evil, but to bring good out of it; to make it the mirror in which His own Eternal Godhead should reflect itself in all its manifold glories.

Reader! These are things that unspeakably concern you. God's purpose is to make more of Himself known to you, a sinner, than was made known to Adam in his sinlessness. He neither shuts Himself out from you, nor you from Himself. He is willing to be known of you; willing to take you into His hidden chambers and reveal Himself to you, as just such a God as a wretched sinner needs. His dealings with you already, in not executing sentence against you, might have taught you this. They contain a story of forbearance and long-suffering, against which it seems strange indeed that you should so madly close your ear. Adam's interruption of the story of God's goodness was nothing to your long-continued refusal to listen to the story of his wondrous patience. To despise goodness is much, but to slight grace is more. To throw away love when once possessed is strangely perverse and ungrateful; but to resolve not to readmit it is more perverse and ungrateful still.

5

How the Story of Grace Began

God's end in overruling Adam's sin embraced many objects, as we have seen. It was a manifold purpose, full of mighty and most varied issues, all of them tending to bring out His whole character in new effulgence; and in unfolding His character, to bless the sinner whose sin had been the occasion of this manifestation.

Yet there was one part of this purpose, more prominent than the rest—that which bore more directly upon man's deliverance. It was grace that was specially to be brought into view. No doubt there were to be new depths of holiness, power, and wisdom, discovered; but it was 'His grace' that was to be the chief object of this new manifestation of God. This, in all its 'exceeding riches,' was now to be revealed. And for this, man's sin afforded the occasion.

But what is grace? Let us understand this fully; for in many ways has this word been mistaken and perverted. It is often on our lips, but how little is its simple reality comprehended!

God loves the angels; He gladdens them with His smiles and blessings, as they wait around His throne, or run at His bidding on their divine errands: but this is not grace. They are obedient and holy; and, as such, love is their natural inheritance. What else could be expected? A holy God must love the holy. God's favour towards the angels proceeds upon the fact that they have no sin. But grace is very different from this. It is still the love of a holy being; but its object is the unholy. The lost, the wretched, the guilty, the worthless, are its sole objects. Under these aspects of sin and ruin alone it contemplates them. Nay, these are the very things which call it forth. It does not go out to the lost, in spite of his being lost, but especially because he is lost. It does not say to the worthless, 'Ah, you are worthless indeed, but I have discovered some fragment of better things about you, and I will show you favour on account of these, notwithstanding your being so worthless.' No, its language is widely different. It is, 'I see you are guilty, wretched, worthless, with nothing in you or about you of what is good; but these are just the very things that I fix upon: they unfit you for everything else, but they do not unfit you for grace.'

It is over the coffin or the tomb of the beloved, that our hearts pour forth the hidden depth of gushing love. So is it over a lost world that the heart of God has gone forth, pouring itself out in all its unutterable tenderness of compassion. It is towards His poor wandering prodigal that the Father's heart goes out. Over him He sighs and weeps. He sees him without a home, without a friend, self-exiled from the paternal roof. He thinks of him in poverty, in rags, in filth, in famine, ready to lie down and die. He fancies him drinking the cup of the drunken, sitting among the unclean, joining in the mirth of the profane, guiltiest among the guilty. And as He broods over these things, His whole heart is turned within Him. He almost forgets the happy circle round Him in the intensity of his yearnings over His outcast boy. So is it with God in His compassion for this forlorn, this self-banished world. The outgoings of His heart towards it are infinitely beyond that of a father's affection, or a mother's deepest tenderness. This is grace— that feeling which is called forth, not by the worth, but by the worthlessness of the object, which awakens at the sight of want, and misery, and guilt; and which can only be gratified by the supply of that want, the removal of that misery, the pardon of that guilt.

Before man sinned, it was only goodness that could show itself—love to the good and worthy. But goodness could no longer find any objects upon earth for its exercise, after sin had entered. Then it was, that when goodness had retired, grace came down, and the story of grace began to be told to man fallen, just as the story of goodness had been told to man unfallen.

When, then, did grace begin? Was it a new feeling that now for the first time arose in the bosom of God? No, grace is from eternity. It is like everything else in God, without a beginning. The fall did not produce some new feeling in Him; it only called forth what had been in Him from everlasting. It supplied new objects—objects of sin and wretchedness—and these brought forth grace into action. But grace is eternal. The story of grace has a beginning; but grace itself has none. We cannot love a friend till we have a friend to love; but the heart which loves has throbbed within us ever since we breathed. We cannot weep over the dead till there are the dead to weep over; but the soul that feels, and the eye that weeps, were not created by the sight of death. It was the sight of the multitudes that awoke the compassion of Jesus; it was the sight of the city that broke up the fountain of his tears: but the tender spirit that commiserates suffering was his always. So it was the sight of sinning, suffering man, that carted forth in Eden the grace of God; but the grace itself had been there during all the infinite past. It was only waiting for an object towards which it might flow out; and now, like a long pent-up river, it burst forth in strength to overflow the earth.

This, then, is the marvel, that man's sin, instead of shutting up the heart of God, and sealing it against the sinner, should be the very thing which unlocks new chambers of its love, and draws forth new stores of its undiscovered and unimagined fulness. It is upon the rain-cloud that light spreads out its sevenfold brilliance; so it was upon man's sin that God began to open out the hidden riches of His infinitely gracious being. It is not the cloudless sky that brings out the whole beauty of earth and heaven; it needs the cloud to open out the treasures of the sunbeam, and to let men see what is contained even in a single ray, so that that which seems to intercept the sunshine is the means of revealing it. And so with the sin of man. It threatened to banish God and goodness from the earth, yet it was the means of bringing Him far nearer than before, and of displaying far more of His goodness, something deeper and more wonderful—*grace*. Thus, it was just 'where sin abounded' that 'grace did much more abound' (Rom. 5:20). Abounding sin drew forth more abounding grace.

This was, indeed, a new aspect of God's character, and it implied a new way of dealing with sin. It was with swift vengeance that He had visited it when it first showed itself in the revolt of the angels. He swept the sin and the sinner clean away. Nor could man expect any other treatment. But God had other thoughts. His purpose was, indeed, still to remove sin, but in another and more glorious way, a way which would exhibit Himself more fully, and, while it condemned sin even more terribly than before, would enable Him to set free the sinner. Formerly, sin and the sinner were dealt with as if inseparable. Wrath unmingled came forth against both. Now they were to be separated. The sin was still to be the object of fiercest wrath, but the sinner was to be the object of grace. How the separation was to be made remained yet to be seen. That there was to be such a separation was early intimated; and the idea of a disjunction between two things hitherto seen as inseparable, was intended to show man in what quarter light was to arise, and where his deliverance lay. Adam could have no idea of being treated differently from the sinning angels; he knew not that sin and the sinner could be separated, or that there could be wrath for the one and grace for the other. The very idea of grace, or free love to the sinner, was new to the universe. Angels could not know it. Their own experience seemed to bear witness against the possibility of such a thing, if, indeed, even the idea of it could arise in their minds.

But God's purpose was to make known this grace to man without delay; the sinner was not long to remain ignorant that there was such a thing as free love in God. The story of grace was begun, and man was called on to listen to it, and learn from it how God could forgive the sinner, and yet be the righteous God.

Reader, there is sin upon you; that sin brings you under condemnation. It makes you an heir of hell. Your rightful portion is the same as that of devils in the lake that burns. But God has revealed His way of separating between the sin and the sinner, a way by which your sin is punished and you are pardoned. Do you know that way? It is the way of grace. If you do not know that way, sin, with its eternal burden, still lies upon your soul. If you know it, and are walking in it, then you have everlasting life, and shall never come into condemnation, but have passed from death unto life (John 5:24). It was the knowledge of this grace that soothed the troubled soul of Adam; and it is the knowledge of this same grace that alone can keep your soul in perfect peace. Many a struggle, many a snare, may lie before you; but the knowledge of this free love will sustain you in all. Through many a sunny, many a stormy hour, you may have to pass; but here is grace suitable for all. 'Be strong in this grace;' keep fast hold of it: it is all to you. Understand it well in all its precious simplicity; mingle nothing with it, else it ceases to be grace: neither add to nor take from it. Receive it just as God has made it known to you. It is sufficient for you to live on, and contains all that is needed to keep your soul in perfect peace. It is a tried spell against the tempter; it is the scatterer of all doubt, the soother of all fear. The knowledge of it will be to you like life from the dead.

6

WHERE THE STORY OF GRACE WAS FIRST TOLD

It was first told in Eden, in the very place where man had broken in upon the story of goodness. It was, indeed, afterwards to be told out of Eden; for man was to be driven forth and the gate closed against him. It was to be told over all the earth, 'to every creature that is under heaven.' But still it was first to be told in Eden. There man had sinned, and there he was to be forgiven; there he had provoked God, and there he was to learn how God could be gracious even to such a rebel.

It was not till he had finished this story of grace that 'He drove out the man.' This is striking, and full of meaning. It is not after the manner of men. No stroke of punishment is to fall on the sinner, no rod of chastisement is to be laid upon him, till he has learned the gracious character of that God whom he had so strangely disobeyed. This, of itself, is grace. Not only is the message a loving one, but the manner, the tone, the time, the place of its delivery, all concur in testifying to the love that it contains. They heighten and enhance the love to which man is now called on to listen.

It would, indeed, have been grace anywhere; though spoken in a dungeon or in a desert, it would still have been grace—grace such as man could not have looked for, yet beyond measure, precious and suitable. Still, when meeting Him upon the very spot where the deed of evil had been done, it wore an aspect of yet deeper mercy. The whole scene bore witness to man's guilt and to the provocation God had received. God could appeal to each object that stood in view, and say, 'What could have been done more to my vineyard that I have not done in it?' (Isa. 5:4). Yet it was here that God revealed forgiveness to the sinner. In the place where all the evidences of his guilt hung around, there mercy overtook him, and made known itself to him. What tenderness is here!

But, besides, thus man's mouth was closed. He could not palliate his guilt by pleading unsupplied wants or unkindly circumstances. He did, indeed, try to throw the blame upon the woman, and through her upon God; but he could go no farther. He could not say, 'Thou hast been to me a wilderness, and a land of darkness' (Jer. 2:31). He could not say, 'Thou hast placed me in most adverse circumstances, thou hast given me nought but a desert to dwell in, and a cold sky for my covering.' He had no ground for such excuses; and the place where he stood, listening to the voice of God, prevented him from making the attempt. 'What iniquity hast thou found in me, that thou hast gone far from me?' (Jer. 2:5), might have been God's words to him. 'What have I done to deserve all this at thy hands? Is this thy kindness to thy friend?'

Thus, grace meets him on the very spot where he stood as a sinner; it takes him just as it finds him, not only a sinner, but trying to cover his sin, and hastening away from God in order to be beyond the reach of His eye. It comes up to him as he stands; it does not wait but hastens to meet him; it does not proclaim itself afar off, but places itself at his very side; it does not require him to come so much of the way to meet it; it goes the whole way to meet him.* It does not call upon him to move one step till it has first taken hold of him; it does not insist upon his obtaining some qualification, some fitness, by throwing off as much of his guilt as he can. It asks for no qualification; it offers to take the whole mass of his guilt at once into its own hand, and to dispose of it in its own way. Such was the fulness, such the absolute freeness, of that grace which was now announced to him in Eden.

Thus has it been ever since. In the place of our sin grace meets us, nay, only there. It was in the land of the Chaldees, the place of his idolatry, that the grace of God met Abraham. He did not come out of Chaldea in order that he might meet with God afterwards in Haran. 'The

---

* An Eastern proverb says, 'If man draws near to God an inch, God will draw near to him an ell.' This is an approach to the truth, yet a poor one; for where should we be if God waited for our 'inch'?

God of glory appeared unto our father Abraham when he was in Mesopotamia, before he dwelt in Charran' (Acts 7:2). It was on the way to Damascus, breathing out slaughter against the saints, that the grace of God met with Saul (Acts 9). It was to the woman caught in the act of sin that the Lord spoke in words of such marvellous grace, 'Neither do I condemn thee; go and sin no more' (John 8:11). In the prison of Philippi, the scene of his hard-heartedness and cruelty to the saints, the grace of God found the poor heathen jailer, and made him to rejoice in God that very night with all his house. It was to the sinners of Jerusalem that the gospel was to be first proclaimed; that, on the very spot where the deed of infinite guilt had been done, there grace might find the doers and tell its glad story in their ears.

Grace does not stand upon the distant mountain top and call on the sinner to climb up the steep heights, that he may obtain its treasures; it comes down into the valley in quest of him; nay, it stretches down its hand into the very lowest depths of the horrible pit, to pluck him thence out of the miry clay. It does not offer to pay the ninety and nine talents, if he will pay the remaining one; it provides payment for the whole, whatever the sum may be. It does not offer to complete the work if he will only begin it by doing what he can. It takes the whole work in hand, from first to last, presupposing his total helplessness. It does not bargain with the sinner that, if he will throw off a few sins and put forth some efforts after better things, it will step in and relieve him of the rest by forgiving and cleansing him. It comes up to him at once, with nothing short of complete forgiveness as the starting point of all his efforts to be holy. It does not say, 'Go and sin no more, and I will not condemn thee,' it says at once, 'Neither do I condemn thee; go and sin no more.'

Indeed, otherwise it would not be grace, but a miserable mixture of grace and merit, a compound of God's doings and man's deservings. If grace does not meet the sinner just where he stands, just as he is, in all his helplessness and guilt, it is no grace to him; for it still leaves an impassable gulf between, a gulf which he has no means to fill up or to cross. If grace wait for anything to be done or felt by man, before it will go forth to him, it will wait forever. If it had waited till Adam came out of the thicket and began to seek after God again, it would never have revealed itself at all. If it had waited till Saul had ceased to hate the master and persecute the disciple, it would never have reached him. If it had waited till Jerusalem had somewhat purged itself from the innocent blood which it had shed, no gospel would ever have been heard within its walls.

Grace of this kind would have been but a mockery to man. If it hang upon some condition to be previously fulfilled, if it insist upon some qualification to be previously obtained, it comes in vain to the sinner; nay, it gives him a stone instead of bread. It points to an ark whose door is shut against him; it tells him of a city of refuge to which he can have no access.

But the grace of God that met Adam in Eden was not such as this. It met him as a sinner, and only as such; it dealt with him as a sinner, and not after he had become something better. This was the only grace that could suit the case of man; it was the only grace that was worthy of God. 'If there be any pardon with God,' says one of another age,

> 'it is such as becomes him to give. When he pardons, he will abundantly pardon. Go with your *half-forgiveness*, limited, conditional pardons, with reserves and limitations, unto the sons of men. It may become them; it is like themselves. That of god is absolute and perfect, before which our sins are as a cloud before the east wind and the rising sun. Hence he is said to do this work with his *whole heart* and with his *whole soul*.'*

Such is the grace that is still going forth to us. It is absolutely and unconditionally free; it comes up to us where we stand; it finds us 'in a desert land, and in a waste howling wilderness.' And there it does its work with us. How little is this understood, especially by the anxious and inquiring! They try to get away from the spot where the guilt was contracted, and where its dark memorials lie thickly scattered on every side. They shrink from dealing with God about forgiveness upon such a spot. They think that God cannot there deal with them in grace, and that to speak of immediate forgiveness to Him in the midst of such a scene would only provoke a repulse, if not His hottest vengeance. Yet it is just there that God meets with

---

*   John Owen on the 130th Psalm.

them, just there that He calls on them to listen to the story of His grace. The effort to escape from that spot, and the wish to deal with God in some less gloomy, less guilty place, are the struggles of self-righteousness. The sense of shame arising from being compassed about with such memorials of sin, and the desire not to appear in the sight of God totally unworthy, are our true reasons for standing aloof from his free grace.

And is not this just the essence of all unbelief—the refusal to own one's self wholly a criminal, and to submit to owe all to grace? And is it not here, at the very outset, that the Holy Spirit's power is so absolutely needed? First, to keep the sinner in the place of guilt, and then to prevent his attempts to shift his ground and to deal with God on some other spot and on some other footing? And then to show him, that though his case be the very worst that God ever dealt with, *grace* is altogether sufficient and exactly suitable?

How often is this the stumbling point with many, whom God is visiting with conviction! They have plunged deep into sin; they have lived as strangers to God, perhaps blasphemers of his name; their life has been one eager chase of pleasure. And when conscience summons them to return from these paths, then they sit down desponding. Their whole course of sin rises up between them and God. They think that the retracing of their steps will be a long, weary process; they do not see it possible that they can deal with God about forgiveness just as they are and just where they stand. They think that they must set about undoing as much as they can of the evil of their former ways before they can transact with God. And hence they too often return in sullen desperation to their former ways.

But is it so, you weary, half-persuaded one, that God will not deal with you as you are? Did He not deal with Adam in the very place of guilt? Did not grace find him there? And is not grace the same? And is not the God of grace the same? You may shrink from his eye; you may say, 'I dare not look upon God as I stand here, in the midst of my sins; I must seek some other less polluted spot where I may meet with him.' But God does not think as you do; He is willing to meet you at this moment, just where you are. And if He is willing, why should you refuse? If He shrinks not from you, why should you shrink from Him? It is your turning away from Him, in whose favour is life, that has embittered your days. And will you not now take His offered hand of welcome, and end all your sorrows in the joy of his endless love?

He is willing to deal with you just now—to have the whole controversy adjusted between you and Him. I do not say He is willing 'to *come* to terms.' He *has come to terms* already, when He bruised His Son upon the cross and made Him our peace. These terms, *already made*, He is now exhibiting to you in the 'gospel of his grace,' that is, the good news about his gracious character as 'the Lord, the Lord God, merciful and gracious, long-suffering, and abundant in goodness and truth, keeping mercy for thousands, forgiving iniquity and transgression and sin' (Exod. 34:6). The sum of these terms is, '*whosoever will,* let him take the water of life *freely*.' Or, in John Bunyan's words, 'The Lord, the governor of the country, hath recorded it in His Book, that if we be truly willing to have it, he will bestow it upon us freely.'

7

By Whom This Story Was Told

It is God Himself who comes down to tell it. He entrusts it to no one else, till He has first announced it. It was too strange a story to be credited from any other messenger. It seemed so incredible, that it must come direct from God, else man might have some ground for giving way to suspicion regarding it. Besides, God wished to be the first to tell His own tale of love.

Man's guilty conscience must have suggested hard thoughts of God. Satan had whispered these already, when, with all the malignity of dark insinuation in his tone, he put the question, 'Yea, hath God said, Ye shall not eat of every tree of the garden?' (Gen. 3:1.) As if he had added, 'What then becomes of the story of His goodness that He has been telling you? Strange goodness this!' These hard thoughts would multiply tenfold, after man yielded to the temptation. The consciousness of guilt would call them up in self-justification. He would palliate the deed that he had done, by making himself believe that God was severe and unkind.

To remove all such thoughts, God Himself comes down. He speaks in person, not through the voice of another. He will leave man without excuse, by letting him hear the story of grace from His own lips. He becomes His own witness, that He may give to man the fullest possible assurance that all this story of grace is really true, and that in His purpose of grace He is entirely sincere. On neither of these points does He afford man any room to doubt. He speaks Himself, and He speaks from His inmost heart. His words are the words of love; they come direct from lips that cannot lie; and the tone in which they are spoken carries irresistible conviction that they are not mere words of course, but the full-hearted utterance of affection.

Little as we think about it, the *tone* of the voice that spoke in the garden must have been most *expressive*. For it was the voice of God—the 'melodious, majestic, mighty voice of God.' In our world of discord, where the heart and the voice are so little in unison, we know something of the expressive power of sounds: though after all it is but little that we know. Yet when someone arises amongst us to whom God has given a voice of melody, and a heart to pour itself through that voice, what influence do the tones of that gifted one wield over us, moving us at will either to weep or smile! And why? Not merely because the sounds were passing sweet; but because they clothed in language, richer and fuller than that of articulate speech, the deep feelings of the soul. When He, then, who formed these sounds, and can wield at pleasure and in truest perfection all their varied power, takes them up and uses as the vehicle of His own divine feelings, how doubly expressive, doubly vocal, would each word become! Thus was it now with Adam when listening to the very voice of God. The words uttered were gracious in themselves, but the tone—the infinitely perfect and expressive tone –carried *in* the words with all-subduing power. It took away every possibility of mistake as to their meaning. We hear it said that some men's voices are more winning and more full of meaning than their words. Was not this supremely true of God? For words must ever be imperfect, seeing they are for the ears and the lips of the finite. But in the varied melody of sound, so ethereal in its very nature, the heart of God can give vent to itself. If anything of God's sincere interest in man's welfare were left unspoken in the words, it would be most fully told by the tones in which these words went forth from the lips of God into the ear of man.

Thus God was his own witness, both by word and by tone. Either of these was enough. Both of them together were irresistible. Can man any longer doubt when it is the voice of God Himself that he hears? How Adam received the blessed announcement we know not. In all likelihood, he listened, believed, and rejoiced. In token of his faith, he called his wife's name Eve, the mother of the living, not of the dead. The lost sheep was brought back, the lost piece of silver recovered, the lost son was found! Alas! That it should not be so always with man, when the glad tidings of the grace of God are proclaimed to him! Strange, that with such a message and with such a witness he should still treat the grace as if it were insincere, and the tidings concerning it as if they were untrue!

And it is just in this strain that God reasons with us, speaking to us by the lips of an Apostle—'If we receive the witness of men, the witness of God is greater' (1 John 5:9). We are ready enough to believe what man says, especially when it is our interest to do so: how much more ready should we be to believe that which is spoken by God! Man has often deceived us, yet we still treat his testimony with confidence. God has never deceived us nor given us cause to suspect his sincerity: with what far greater confidence should we treat his testimony!

Yet the fact is otherwise. We are much more ready to believe man than God; nay, more ready to believe Satan than God. We have no assurance that man is our friend, yet we believe him; we know that Satan is our enemy, as also the father of lies, yet we believe him. God has never given us any ground to think ill of Him, yet we refuse to receive His witness when He testifies to us of the 'riches of his grace.' Is not this strange and sad? Is it not most unreasonable and perverse? It could not be credited were it not manifested every day before our eyes. If the story of God's grace amazes us, the story of man's unbelief may astonish us far more.

It is with this unreasonableness that God taxes us. He appeals to us respecting the perversity of our conduct.

'You listen to your fellow men, why will you not listen to Me? You transact the daily business of your lives in faith upon your neighbours, why will you not transact the business of eternity in faith upon Me? Am I the only one whose word is not to be taken, whose testimony is to be suspected?' Thus God condescends to reason with us, when He might righteously have thrust us away without a word of entreaty. In so doing, He brings out our treatment of Him in its darkest aspect, and, by the way in which He puts it, leaves us inexcusable. For had we not been in the habit of believing anyone, we might have had some pretext for our distrust—some plea of self-justification in this course of unbelief. But when we so continually and so readily 'receive the witness of man,' we are without excuse if we refuse or suspect the witness of God, which is so much surer and stronger.

It was with this unbelief that Christ charged Israel— 'If I say the truth, why do ye not believe Me?' It is with this unbelief that God charges the world—'They received not the love of the truth that they might be saved.' And it is on this point that He so solemnly warns us—'Take heed lest there be in any of you an evil heart of unbelief in departing from the living God.' It was this evil heart of unbelief that drew Adam away from God. It is this same heart of unbelief that still keeps His children away. It is not the greatness of their sins, for God is willing to bury them all out of sight. It is the evil heart of unbelief! It was this that kept Israel out of Canaan and made them perish in the wilderness. It is this that keeps men out of the better Canaan and consigns them to the abyss of woe.

For unbelief is that which most displeases and dishonours God. It is the denial of the story of his grace; nay, it is the belief of something else in its stead—the belief of a lie. It is a defacing of God's image; it is a blackening of God's character; it is a refusal of His friendship; it is a preference of self and the world to Him; it is a deliberate rejection of His Son, and of the gift of life in Him. For every moment's delay in receiving this gift implies far more than mere indifference or neutrality, it implies a distinct and positive rejection! With this dark guilt, God charges the world; and with this we now charge every unbelieving soul that reads these pages. I enter here into no question as to the absolute necessity of the Holy Spirit's inward work upon the soul in order to believing. I simply charge you, upon the authority of God, with this wilful unbelief, this deliberate rejection of His infinite gift. It is at your peril that you attempt to excuse yourself for one moment's continuance in unbelief. Your doing so is but adding guilt to guilt; and you cannot really suppose it possible that there is any one to blame for your unbelief but yourself, or that there is any sufficient reason for your remaining in that state another hour.

The line that God draws is between those who receive His witness and those who receive it not. All who receive it have eternal life and shall never come into condemnation. All who do not receive it are condemned already and are ripening for the everlasting condemnation hereafter. They who are listening to His story of grace, and receiving it as little children do the story of a mother's love, are members of His heavenly family, and heirs of His kingdom. They who are closing their ears against it, and listening to the world's flatteries, or Satan's falsehoods, are exiles from His favour, and inheritors of a wrath that shall burn unabated forever.

On which side of this line are you, reader? I do not ask on which side of it you *hope to be* at death; but on which side of it you *are* at this moment. There is life on the one side and death on the other. Which of these two is your *present* portion? Does the line seem a narrow one, and do you think it hard that the abiding on one side of it should be death, and strange that by crossing it you should be landed on the shore of life? Remember that it is God, not man, who draws the line. And who will attempt to alter the boundary which He marks out?

Nor is it, after all, an arbitrary line. This belief is the belief of all that is gracious and glorious in the character of God, and consequently of all that is fitted to make you truly blessed. This unbelief, on the other hand, is the shutting out of all this wondrous display of God's infinite nature; nay, it is the positive belief of that which is opposed to this. Do you still wonder, then, why such momentous consequences should hang on your belief or your unbelief? How can it be otherwise, in the very nature of things? Do you ever ask why the enjoyment or deprivation of day's refreshing light should depend upon the opening or the closing of these slender eyelids of yours? Do you ask why the churchyard or the charnel house* is so gloomy and saddening, and why summer-fields are so joyous to the heart? Do you ask why there should be such gladness in meeting and such pain in parting with those we love? Do you ask why it is so sweet to love and to be loved, and so terrible to hate and to be hated? No. You do not call these things arbitrary. Yet you know them simply as facts of your nature—nothing more. Their how and why are beyond your stretch. They belong to the deep and undiscovered harmonies of being. He only can follow them out who has seen the plan of the universe and, having seen it, has mastered all its details, looking round upon the whole from the same centre from which the Eternal Architect beheld them when He first planned the vast design.

Or does all this seem to make the blessings too free? Do you say, 'If it be all of grace, and if we are to get life on such easy terms, what then becomes of morality, and of the law, and of a holy life?' The answer is, these are all provided for—and far more fully provided for in the way of grace than in any other plan they could have been.†

---

*   A vault or building in which corpses or human skeletal remains are stored.

†   He turned to the woman—turned with a look of pardoning mercy—'Thy sins are forgiven thee.' Observe, the Divine Redeemer says not one word of a new life, of self-government, of moral restraint. And why? Because he knew that she loved much; and he knew that love knows of no sorrow for sin, which does not lead to forsaking of sin; and though man might think that the pardoned sinner would never again bestow one thought upon his past sins, he knew that it is *after* pardon that the sinner begins to see them as they really are—begins to know them in all their enormity—

Nay, this is the only way in which the ends of holiness can be served, and the fulfilment of the law secured. For the law is the law of love, not of fear. The only true keeping of it is the keeping of it in love. The motives for keeping it must be addressed to our hearts as well as to our consciences. They must be motives appealing to what is loving and generous in the soul; not grounded on constraint or terror, or the suspense of a doubtful forgiveness. If a man is made to wait and work for pardon, there cannot but be constraint, and terror, and uncertainty. Thus, the affections are frozen—the heart has no room to play. In other words, the law *cannot* be kept at all. The feet may move in the direction to which terror impels, but that is the utmost.

The only way to have this law of love kept by the sinner, is to send him a free forgiveness, to assure him of free love, to put him in possession of the free favour of God—to do all this at once, without delay, without waiting, without working, without uncertainty, without suspending wrath over him.

And how can this be done save in *believing*? If *working* be necessary, it cannot be done. 'It is of faith that it might be of grace.' A sin-bearer is made known to us—the good news concerning his sin-bearing are proclaimed to us; and, in believing these, we have immediate pardon. We are not kept in suspense; 'we *have* peace with God.' The reconciliation is at once effected. What, then, flows from

begins to weep for them, because committed against a God so ready to pardon and so slow to anger.—From the Italian of Girolamo Fornielli.

this? Love to God, and a desire to do His will: love to the law, and a delight in keeping it—a longing after entire conformity to God Himself. How simple and how blessed! Surely He who framed the Gospel knew our nature well. He knew the hearts which He had made, and how to touch their springs. And, therefore, in order that we may keep the law of love, He introduces love at the very outset. Terror could not do this. Suspense could not make a man holy. An uncertain forgiveness could not unlock our fetters.

Thus, the gospel is no arbitrary thing, but most natural as well as most simple—the only thing which can furnish sufficient motives to a holy life—the only thing that can call forth in us the response of happy confidence and childlike love. They who revile a free gospel as the inlet to licentiousness, show that they understand neither the gospel nor the law. They know not man's nature, nor how to touch the springs of the heart. Holiness with them is the fruit of compulsion, and terror, and dreary suspense. They would secure it by making pardon a blessing to be strenuously worked for, and only earned after a lifetime's obedience or penance. Holiness with God is the freed soul pouring itself out in a life of loving obedience.* He secures

---

*   'If any man ask me, seeing that faith justifieth me, why I work, I answer, *love compelleth me.* For as long as my soul feeleth what love God hath showed me in Christ, I cannot but love God again, and his will and commandments, and of love do them; nor can they seem hard unto me.'—Tyndale's *Bible: Preface to Exodus.*

'Sin is the disease. What is the remedy? Charity? Nonsense. Charity is the health, the state to be obtained by the use of the remedy, not the

it by the gift of free and entire forgiveness, which becomes ours simply in believing the testimony of His grace as set before us in the cross of His beloved Son.

---

sovereign balm itself—faith of grace, faith in the God-manhood, the cross, the mediation, the perfected righteousness of Jesus, to the utter rejection and abjuration of all righteousness of our own. Faith alone is the restorative. The Romish scheme is preposterous: it puts the rill before the spring. Faith is the source—charity, that is, the whole Christian life, is the stream from it.'—Coleridge, *Literary Remain.*

8

The Outline of the Story

Not knowing anything of grace, nor how such a thing could be, Adam fled from God. He was afraid of God, and of His anger, for the hope of forgiveness could not enter his mind. He was ashamed to meet with God, for the sense of unfitness to stand in His presence would possess him. An evil conscience told him that God must now be his enemy, and that he had no favour to look for at his hands. Free love had not yet been made known, and the idea of it could not originate with the creature. It must originate with God. He alone could tell how such a thing could be, and He alone could suggest it to man.

Accordingly, when man fled, God followed. He was eager to escape from God, and to get as far as possible out of His sight. The presence of God had become as terrible as it had once been blessed. God overtook him among the trees. Search was immediately made for sin. It was found upon the man. God began with Adam, for with him, as the head of creation, he had hitherto been dealing. This same sin was then traced back to the woman and charged also against her. It was then traced backward further still to the serpent. Step by step it was thus tracked out, and laid open to view in all its windings—a specimen this of God's procedure in the day of judgment, when He shall lay bare all sin, and hold it up to the abhorrence of the universe.

When the fountainhead of the evil had thus been reached, the sentence was pronounced. The search for sin had begun with Adam, but the sentence against it began with the serpent, as the origin of the whole. It seemed a sentence of wrath, but it was truly one of grace. It spoke of death, but life was in it. It was the first ray of light beginning to dawn upon the world, over which man's disobedience had drawn so dark a cloud. It was not spoken directly to Adam, but simply in his hearing, that he may feel that this grace and life do not arise from any good thing in him, but from God's mere pity towards him, and from His desire to undo the evil which had been wrought.

The sentence against the serpent assures us that God has taken man's part against the enemy that had ruined him. Thus much of grace could be seen at once in it. God steps in between man and his seducer, expressing his displeasure against that which had been done to man. 'Thou hast done this,' are his words of condemnation against the adversary. He then lays the curse on Satan, and predicts his final overthrow, notwithstanding his present victory. This was grace. Still further, He promises a seed to the woman, and this was special grace; for it told her that the sentence of death was not immediately to overtake her. She was to *live;* and, through her, deliverance was to find its way to the race. Through this seed Satan's ruin was to come. Between the woman and the serpent there was to be no longer friendship, but enmity. They had been companions in sin, accomplices in crime, but they were henceforth to be at enmity. Nay, between the two seeds there was to be deadly conflict carried on, ending in victory to the woman's seed, but not without the bruising of his heel; nay, by means of this very bruising. All this was grace; each word was expressive of some gracious design on the part of God, on behalf of the sinner. God's purpose of grace was thus intimated, though not unfolded.

Yet it was grace arising out of, or, at least, founded on God's hatred of sin. The first words God utters in the ears of man are such as to show him that, whatever that grace might be, it was grace such as could only reach him in a way expressive of this hatred. Sin was to be treated as an infinite evil, not as a thing which God could pass slightly over, or to which He could be indifferent. Men sometimes speak of grace as if it had its origin in God's indifference to sin. But, at the very outset, God would have us know that this cannot be. Grace can only come forth in the way of recognising sin's utter hatefulness—a hatefulness so great, that the one way of removing or pardoning sin is by God's taking the treatment of it entirely into his own hands. And thus it is still. Grace can only be understood when taken in connection with the 'exceeding sinfulness of sin,' and the entire unworthiness of the sinner. If sin be not altogether evil, and if the sinner be not altogether worthless, then grace becomes a word without a meaning. Hence it is that self-righteousness and grace are totally incompatible with each other; so that, the moment we begin to palliate our sin, in order to obtain forgiveness, we are falling from grace. As soon as we begin to look for some good feeling or deed in us, in order to make us less unfit to apply to God for pardon, we are rejecting grace. When we allow doubts to arise in us on account of the greatness or the frequency of our sins, we are losing sight of grace. When we try to get or to regain peace in any way which supposes that we are less than the chief of sinners, we are misunderstanding grace, and refusing to acknowledge what it must always rest upon—that sin's malignity is unspeakable, and God's hatred of it unchangeable. And this was evidently in the mind of the Lord when He said, 'I came not to call the righteous, but sinners to repentance.' The grace, which He came to announce, was grace which had nothing to do with man in any other character save that of a sinner.

Thus God's gracious character began to show itself. It was plain that He had now taken the side of man against his great enemy, and thus manifested His grace as distinctly as He did to Israel when He said, 'I will be an enemy unto thine enemies, and an adversary unto thine adversaries.' He had so espoused man's cause as to place Himself between him and his adversary, declaring war against the serpent and its seed forever, but proclaiming no war against man, nay, implying a restoration to friendship, for it was the seed of the woman that He meant to make the instrument of His victory over Satan.

This was much indeed. It was a reprieve, at least, if it was nothing more. It suspended the sentence if it did not revoke it. But it did more than this. It intimated the grace or free love that His bosom contained—a free love which seemed resolved to proceed onwards in the attainment of its object—that would grudge no cost, nor toil, nor sacrifice, in order to its attainment. There was indeed as yet but a dim and partial revelation of grace, but it was enough to show Adam, that however much God hated the sin that had been done, He had not become the implacable enemy of man, but was willing to befriend and bless him still. Man might still enjoy His friendship, though a sinner; man might yet taste God's love, though he had made himself so utterly unlovable. He may take himself to the God that made him, and find shelter beneath the shadow of His wings, nay, gladness in the embrace of His everlasting arms. He need not avoid his creator, as if there were nought but destruction and terror in His presence. Man had indeed altered his condition, but there was something in God to meet that altered condition. What God had formerly manifested of Himself could not meet it; but now He had come down to intimate that there was that very thing in Him which this changed state required, and that this thing was not wrath, but *grace.*

This was the first *ray* of returning light. It was not the sun; that was not to rise for ages. Neither was it the morn. But it was the first streak of brightness upon the overhanging clouds. It foretold the dawn; it was the sure forerunner of the sun. The clouds did not forthwith depart—the curse did not leave the earth—man's restoration was not complete. But it was clearly intimated that the process was now begun through which all these would be accomplished. Satan was not to triumph; sin was not to have its way unhindered; God's favour was now made sure. This was enough—the rest would follow in due time. And what might man not hope for, if God's favour were restored? That would brighten all darkness and turn all sorrow into joy.

These were the tidings of grace—the story of free love that Adam heard. And news like these were just what his case required. They arrested him in his flight from God, for they told him how much he had mistaken the character of the God he was fleeing from, and they made him feel that his safety lay not in escaping from God, but in returning to Him. They made his fig leaves fall from off him, for they told him of a far better clothing, a covering made by the hands of God. They won his heart, they relieved his doubts, they stilled all his alarms, while they at the same time made him thoroughly ashamed of his sin. They gently drew him out of the thick shades in which he had sought to hide himself from the face of God. Terror and threatening could not have done this; they would only have made him clasp his fig leaves the more firmly and driven him further away to hide himself in deeper shades. But this unexpected, yet most blessed discovery of grace, spoke peace to his soul. It told him that God was still willing to be his friend—still ready to welcome him back to his paternal bosom.

Nothing is prescribed for him to do in order to secure God's favour or get the benefit of the good news. They are made known to him by God. The story of free love is told, or, at least, sketched in outline. He listens—he sees that it is God Himself who is speaking, and that, therefore, there can be no deception. He gives God credit for speaking truly; he believes, and peace re-enters his soul. The story of love thus taught him outwardly by the hearing of the ear, and taught him inwardly, at the same moment, by the Holy Ghost, was all he needed to pacify his conscience and to gladden his heart.

Nor was there any room left for suspicion or doubt. Man seemed shut up to believe and to trust. One would have said that no door for unbelief was left open, and that the difficulty would not be, to believe, but to keep from believing. It was not much, indeed, that was said, but that little was enough to show Adam that God was altogether such a one as he, a sinner, could trust in. To suspect or to doubt Him, then, was to say that there was not enough of grace in Him for such a sinner, or that there was not grace of the particular kind he needed. This was, in fact, to cast discredit upon that very revelation of God's character which had just been made.

However briefly the message had been spoken, it left man inexcusable if he persisted in cherishing aught like a doubt. For to whatever extent sin had gone, there was grace made known more than sufficient to meet it. To whatever depth of unworthiness the character of man might be sunk, still there stood God, making Himself known in that very character which was fitted to suit even the unworthiest; so that every doubt that might arise from a sense of personal unworthiness was at once answered; nay, it was so answered as to be shown to be, not really a sense of unworthiness in himself, but a disbelief or denial that there was sufficient grace in God to meet that unworthiness. Nay, more, it could be nothing else than pride refusing to owe such a debt to God; and this not so much arising from a feeling of unworthiness, as from the disappointment of not being allowed to present anything of his own goodness to God as a recommendation to favour.

Reader, you have here the commencement of God's story of grace. It is the truest and the most blessed that was ever told. In it there are no exaggerations, no descriptions of fancy. It is all reality—the reality of immeasurable love. It is spoken as directly and personally to you as it was to Adam. It is not merely a message to your first parent, out of which his children may ingeniously contrive to extract or pilfer something which does not rightly belong to them. It is a message to you, and on the reception which you give to that message your forgiveness and your blessedness depend.

What reception, then, do you mean to give it? It is God who tells this story of love—will you listen to Him and allow His loving words to drop as the rain, and to distil as the dew? All that He asks is that you would listen. 'Hear, and your souls shall live.' You have listened to many a speaker; will you not listen to the God that made you? You have listened to many a tale of earthly love; will you not for once, at least, listen to the tale of heavenly love? The tales of earth but vitiate the taste, and enervate the spirit, nay, perhaps, corrupt your whole moral being. This tale has divine healing in its every word. It soothes, it refreshes, it gladdens, and it leaves no sting, no weariness behind. Is it not, then, worth your while to listen? You have heard the outline—it is full of grace. And if the mere outline be so exquisite, what must be the filling up of that wondrous tale which began to be sketched in Eden, which was told more fully by prophets and apostles, which is still continuing to be told throughout the earth, and yet, with regard to which we may say, that the half remains untold? The 'ages to come' must tell it.

9

THE CONQUEROR

The question had now been answered, 'Is there *grace* in God to man the sinner?' There is grace, was God's own announcement.

But how is this to be carried out? There may be free love in God, and a most sincere desire to bless, but what if righteousness forbid these to flow down? How are they to get vent to themselves, so that man may partake of them? Can the separation be so made between sin and the sinner, that the one may be condemned and the other acquitted; the one made the object of the curse, the other of the blessing? God has answered this question also. He has told that there is a way, a righteous way, of accomplishing this. That way is through the intervention of *the woman's seed*. It is through Him that this righteous adjustment of the claims of law is to be made. He is to give the law its due, and yet let the transgressor go free.

There are three things regarding Him of which we get a glimpse in this first promise. First, He is to be the seed of the woman. Second, He is to be bruised in the heel. Third, He is to bruise the head of the serpent. In other words, He is to be *a man, a sufferer, a conqueror.*

He is to be a man.

One 'born of a woman;' a being of flesh and blood. Yet evidently more than a man, for He is to deliver man; more also than an angel, for He is to be the destroyer of Satan. A man, and yet more than a man; a man, and yet greater and mightier than man's angelic foe! This is the brief and mysterious, yet most comprehensive description of the deliverer's person, which God vouchsafed to Adam. *A man, and yet more than a man*—this was the first great idea of the conqueror which God revealed, and on which He left Adam to meditate, till, having turned it on every side, and sought to fathom the mystery, he was prepared for hearing more.

Still that little was much. It did—what God throughout all Scripture is doing—turned man's eye to a person, not a thing—to a person, not a truth. How truly, and how powerfully, has one in our own day written of this:

> The prerogative of our Christian faith, the secret of its strength, is that all which it has, and all which it offers, is laid up in a person. This is what has made it strong, when so much else has proved weak, that it has a cross as its middle point; that it is not a circumference without a centre; that it has not merely

a deliverance, but a deliverer; not a redemption only, but a redeemer as well. This is what makes it fit for wayfaring men; this is what makes it sunlight, and all else compared with it but as moonlight: fair it may be, but cold and chill; while here the light and the life are one; the Light is also the Life of men. Oh! How great the difference between submitting ourselves to a complex of rules, and casting ourselves upon a beating heart—between accepting a system and cleaving to a person!*

He is to be a sufferer.

He is to be bruised, yet not in any vital part, so as to terminate His being. His bruise is to be in an inferior member. Yet still it is a bruise. He is to suffer. There was to be enmity, nay, conflict; and in that conflict He was to be wounded. This wounding is evidently a most important point. Adam's eye must have been drawn to this, as something wonderful, something mysterious, in this promised seed. If He is to be Satan's conqueror, why is He bruised? Must not this bruising be necessary? Is it not through this bruising that victory is to come? The *words* here, plainly announced that this suffering was to be *for our benefit*; the *sacrifices*, which were immediately instituted, told that it was to be *in our stead*. Deliverance by *substitution* was thus early revealed, that thus far at least, there might be no mistake. It was the *bruised* seed of the woman that was to be man's deliverer; and this bruising was to be such as the sacrifice pointed to, and for the same

---

*   Trench's *Hulsean Lectures* for 1846, p. 122.

end. The bruising and the sacrifice were to be associated together; and, thus associated, they each cast light upon the other.

And is not this that very truth in which we now rejoice? A deliverer that has suffered? One whose suffering avails to avert suffering from us; nay, one whose suffering is to take the place of our suffering? In other words, it is not merely a suffering *benefactor* that is revealed, but a *suffering* substitute—one who, possessing all that we are lacking in, changes place with us, that we may get all that belongs to Him, He taking all that belongs to us. It was thus that, in 1512, Lefevre spoke from amid the darkness of the University of Paris: 'O, unutterable exchange! The sinless One is condemned, the guilty goes free; the Blessed bears the curse, the cursed bears the blessing; the Life dies, and the dead live; the Glory is covered with shame, and the shame is covered with glory!'

In the promise itself, these things might be dimly seen; but when the sacrifice and the promise were placed side by side, what light arose! That lamb upon the altar spoke of the bruised one, foreshadowing His suffering and His work. In looking to the lamb, Adam was looking to this bruised one. And, in looking, his conscience was pacified, his soul was comforted. It was what he saw in that bruised heel that removed his fears and drew him once more close to the side of God. This man shall be 'our peace,' was the inscription which his eye could read upon the altar. This suffering one was he who was to embody all grace, as well as to reveal it; nay, to be the channel through which that grace was to find its way to man, as 'the grace that bringeth salvation.'

He is to be a conqueror.

He was to fight our battles, as well as to pay our penalties. There was a fierce enemy to war with, or rather a thick array of enemies. Against these He was to stand alone. Taking hold of shield and buckler, He was to stand up for our help. For a while the battle was to remain doubtful, but not long. The victory and the triumph were to be His; and, if His, then also ours. Nor were these to be but partial; they were to be complete and final. The *head* of the enemy was to be bruised.

But why was there even a momentary advantage gained by Satan? Why was there anything like wounds or weakness seen in this mighty conqueror? Because righteousness stood up against Him, and demanded that, since He had undertaken the cause of the unrighteous, He should allow their penalty to be exacted of Him. For it was the cause of the unrighteous He had come to maintain, though not the cause of unrighteousness. With the latter He could have nought to do; the former was the object of His errand. Thus, righteousness fought against Him and prevailed, till it was fully satisfied. Then it ceased, and Satan had no longer this upon his side. The law, too, fought against Him, and prevailed, till its claims were settled in full. Then it was silent. And Satan was deprived of this ally also. Law and righteousness being thus taken out of Satan's hands, so that they could no longer be used by him against this mighty one, forthwith His triumph began, and Satan's overthrow was secured. The only hope of victory to the enemy, lay in having righteousness upon his side in the conflict. This weapon he wielded to the utmost, little knowing that in so doing he was really striking it out of his own hands, nay, turning it in upon his own vitals. At every stroke, this righteousness, which was the only thing that made him strong, was getting itself satisfied, till, when the last stroke was given, and the victim fell prostrate in death, as if Satan had overcome, righteousness, now completely vindicated in all its claims, changed sides. Satan's ally was gone, and he was left helpless to battle with the whole unhindered strength of the mighty warrior.

Then the victory was secure. Satan's brief success was the beginning of defeat and shame. Righteousness was now upon the side of the woman's seed; and if on His, then on ours. Law now also stood up on His side; and if on His, then on ours. Thus, He won the day; and won it for us. Those very things which fought against us were now turned to fight for us. He has made it entirely according to *law*, that a sinner should be saved and Satan robbed of his prey. He has made it not only a gracious, but a righteous thing in God to welcome the sinner back, and clasp him in the embrace of love.

But the *whole* victory is not yet secured. The enemy is not yet driven from the field, nor all his victims wrested from his grasp. The process is going on just now, and every sinner who is willing to take this conquering one for his champion, and enrol himself as His, becomes part of the rescued spoil. Yet the war shall not cease till this conqueror appear the second time, to bind the enemy, to undo the evil that he has done, to seize the residue of the prey, to deliver the groaning earth, to bid Eden re-blossom in an atmosphere no longer poisoned by the breath of hell.

Thus has the 'horn of salvation been raised up for us,' and God's purpose carried out, 'that we should be saved from our enemies, and from the hand of all that hate us,' (Luke 1:69-71). The man, the sufferer, the conqueror, has appeared—the woman's seed, the second Adam, who is the Lord from heaven. *Now*, then, we know of a truth, that God has so loved the world as to give His only-begotten Son; that Christ Jesus, the seed of the woman and the Son of God, 'has appeared to put away sin by the sacrifice of Himself;' that He has been 'Once offered to bear the sins of many; and that to them that look for him shall he appear the second time without sin unto salvation' (Heb. 9:26-28).

It is this man, this sufferer, this conqueror, that presents Himself to us, 'full of grace and truth.' He has done His work; and He asks us to come and share its fruits. He has conquered; and He asks us to partake of His triumph. To each one of us He holds out the friendly hand, offering to lead us into that paradise which He has reopened, and which now stands before us with unfolded gates.

It is this man, this sufferer, this conqueror, that God is pointing to, as He in whom it has pleased Him that all fulness of grace should dwell. The story of grace has not only been told in words, but embodied in a person, the person of the God-man, the woman's seed. In Him there is represented and contained 'the manifold grace of God'—the 'exceeding riches of his grace.' It is not *words* that God has given us; it is far more than this. It is not abstract truth that He places before us. It is a person, a living person, a man like ourselves, that He sets before us, as the vessel in which all this truth is contained. He clothes His grace in the loving form of manhood; He makes it to beam forth from a loving countenance; He gives it utterance through a loving voice; He sends it to tell its own story to us, in deeds that are without a parallel from the beginning of the world. It is this God-man, in whom all grace is stored, that invites you to enjoy His blessings. All the day long He stretches out His hands. His message is, 'Come unto me, and I will give you rest;' and lest you should hesitate or fear, He adds, 'Him that cometh unto me I will in no wise cast out.'

May He not, then, expect you to regard him, when thus pleading with you to yield to his beckoning hand and allow Him to lead you to blessedness? This much at least he might surely count upon, when your own interests for eternity are the matters on which He is so urgent and importunate. Especially when all is a free gift. No merit, no money, no prerequisite on your part is asked for. Everything is already *bought*; bought by *His* deservings, and therefore not needing to be bought over again by *yours*. May He not, then, expect that you should take His gift;—nay, take it with ready and eager gladness? May He not wonder at your refusal? What! Refuse eternal life! Reject a kingdom! And in their stead take death, and shame, and weeping as your portion? Prefer an eternity of darkness to an eternity of light! Turn away from an open paradise and choose the desolation of the everlasting wilderness! Does not all this seem incredible, impossible?

Meanwhile the day is wearing on. The shadows of the night, that has no morn beyond it, are falling down upon you. 'There is sorrow on the sea, and it cannot be quiet' (Jer. 49:23). The world is growing old; and the cry of its transgression is going up, like the cry of Abel's blood, demanding speedy vengeance. That cry must soon be heard. For the sole reason of delay is the long-suffering of God, 'not willing that any should perish, but that all should come to repentance' (2 Pet. 3:9). Had it not been for this longsuffering, this marvellous patience of God, the fire would long since have seized upon this rebellious earth.

What, then, are you to do, who are still unsaved and unsheltered? Will pleasure be pleasure then; or will it not be gall and wormwood? Will the world's gay glitter continue then to bewilder you? Where will be the spell of its beauty, the music of its siren song? They 'are not:' and 'in one hour thou art made desolate.' Its blossoms have gone up as dust; and its joys are forgotten dreams. The freshness of youth has faded; the ties of kindred are broken; the gladness of companionship is at an end; the greetings of neighbourhood have ceased; the voices of home are silent; and the old familiar melodies of earth have died away. All have been 'covered with a cloud' in the day of the fierce anger of the Lord! And for you, unsaved one, there remains nought but the everlasting darkness, which no star will gladden, and on which no hope will arise. The judgment seemed long in coming; you were hoping that it would never arrive. But it has come at last. And its coming is the final quenching of all hope for you! The Judge that long stood before the door (James 5:9) at length makes His entrance. And is not that entrance the sealing of your doom? He had long patience with you; but you would not give heed; and now His patience is turned into wrath; and that wrath turns all your hope into despair.

10

THE BANISHED ONE

'He drove out the man.' Perhaps man lingered, unwilling to leave so fair a dwelling. But he must abide there no longer. God's purpose is that Eden shall not be his home. Therefore, He *drove* him out.

He is banished from Eden, the place where God had set His glory. Sin has interposed between him and God. There is distance, not nearness, now. The promise, which he took along with him, assured him that he had not been cast off; that there would be restoration: but meanwhile there was to be distance. There were obstacles which required to be surmounted before the sinner could draw nigh. His expulsion showed that these had not yet been removed, that the way into the presence of God, 'the holiest of all,' was not yet laid open. Thus was proclaimed to him the awful truth, 'Your iniquities have separated between you and your God; it is sin that has broken up the intercourse; it is sin that has cast you out of Eden:

you have done all this with your own hand; it is not God's doing, but your own; you have made yourself a wanderer, and transformed earth into a wilderness.'

Yet there was *grace*, too, in this expulsion. It was not a sentence executed against a criminal; it was chastisement inflicted on a son. Nay, it was in tender mercy towards him, lest he should put forth his hand and eat the fruit of the tree of life. For as the food plucked from the other trees was intended to nourish the body, so this was designed to nourish the immortal principle. In saying that the principle of immortality required nourishment, I do not mean that man was created mortal as he now is, any more than I mean this, when I say that he needed food even in paradise to sustain his body. But still the eating of the tree of life was to *preserve* his immortality;—not to produce it, but to preserve it. Now God's purpose is that it should not be preserved, but that man should die and return to dust. And this was not merely that, in great kindness, he might make a sad life a brief one, but because God had a better life in reserve for him, which could only be reached by passing through death. This was *life in resurrection*.

God's design was to bring man, through death, to resurrection-life. This was a far superior life—life upon a higher scale, and endued with higher properties. God was from this time to fix man's eye upon *resurrection*, not immortality in the present body, as his true hope. He wished to connect all blessings, material and immaterial, with this hope of resurrection. And thus, in mercy he withdrew man from the tree of life and sent him forth to die. Everything in creation must be taken to pieces—down to the very foundation—that it may be rebuilt of far nobler materials, and after a far more glorious model. Man might have desired the life without death; but God, in wise compassion, would not suffer it to be so. His desire was to give him a better life—life through death—incorruption coming from corruption, immortality springing from the grave.

Thus man's eye was fixed upon the life beyond death, the life that was to spring out of death, the life of resurrection. Had he not been shut out from the tree of life, had he not been sent forth to die, he would have been contented with the life without death. But God had provided some better thing for him; and to that better thing he now turned his eye when he was driven beyond the reach of the tree of life. Resurrection was now his hope. Death lay before him, but resurrection lay beyond it. 'Dust thou art, and unto *dust* shalt thou return,' was the sentence. But his banishment from Eden would help him in some measure to anticipate, however dimly, the resurrection promise, 'Awake and sing, ye that dwell in *dust*.'

Besides this, he was now to be called to a life of faith. God's purpose was to teach him how 'blessed they are who have not seen, and yet have believed.' All had been sight hitherto; now all was to be faith. Sight had told him much of God; but faith was to tell him far more. He had known the sweetness of walking with God in the day of his unfallen strength; he was now to know the deeper blessedness of leaning upon God, in the day of sorrowing helplessness. The deep waters through which he was to pass would require more of God's resources to be drawn out. These man was to taste in all their fulness. New wants in himself were to be the means of calling out new supplies from God. Grace was now to get a thousand channels through which to pour itself along. The very ills of his lot were to become inlets of heavenly blessing.

He was also to be taught, that henceforth all the intercourse between him and God was to be upon a new footing—that of grace alone. His banishment was the constant memorial of this. Why was he now outside of Eden? Because he was a sinner. But why still preserved and not consigned to wrath? Because there is grace for the sinner. All he tasted now was of grace. God's gifts were not withheld, but they were bestowed in grace. He stood upon a new footing altogether; and every step he took reminded him of this. A lost Eden, but a saved sinner; these two conjoined, were the daily preachers of grace. God was still his God, though not in Eden. And thus, though he felt himself a banished man, he could rejoice in forgiveness. The consciousness that he was a sinner, was not to mar his peace, or to come between him and his God. Grace had made up the breach; but it had done so in a way which continued to remind him that nothing but grace could have done it. God had been with him in Eden, and He was still with him when expelled from it. Though God could not meet with him in the spot where they had met before, yet He was willing to meet with him outside these 'happy seats.'

Yes, God was still his God, though out of Eden. There had been a moment of separation—after the sin had been committed, and before the promise was given. That moment of suspense must have been terrible to Adam, like a glance into the abyss. But now that was over, grace had been revealed, and God was again his God. He was a banished man, and earth was to be a desert to him; but God was to be with him, and he could bear the loss of paradise. I know not if ever this feeling was more truly expressed than in the following lines of the great poet of England. They refer to human love; but we may use them in a nobler sense:—

> 'Tis not the land I care for, wert *thou* hence:
> A wilderness is populous enough
> So I had but thy heavenly company:
> For where thou art, there is the world itself,
> With every several pleasure in the world;
> And where thou art not—desolation.

Thus man was sent forth as a stranger and a pilgrim. He was not a wanderer, a fugitive, like Cain. Still he was to be a stranger. For the promise had lifted his eye beyond things seen and temporal, to the things unseen and eternal. He looked for the better, the enduring substance. Whatever the darkness of the way might be, however many might be the centuries of mortal life that lay in sorrow before him, still it was a joy to think that this was not his rest. His home and heritage were not on this side of the tomb. And as it was through death that he was passing to his better life, so it was through exile that he was to pass to the land which was to be his forever. It might be a second paradise, or the same paradise restored. It might be something far different. That mattered not. It would be a sufficient home for him, if it was the home allotted by his forgiving God. Nay, would it not be worthy of that grace that had already disclosed such wonders to him? Would it not be worthy of the God of grace; so that God should 'not be ashamed to be called his God'? Deep consolation this to one who had 'destroyed himself,' who had blighted Eden and ruined a world!

And what are we but banished men—born outside of Eden, and breathing only the air of the wilderness? This is our lot, our birthright, as children of this first banished one. Perhaps we have become so familiar with the desert, as to look with an easy, it may be, a satisfied eye, upon its rocky barrenness. Still this cannot change the awful truth that we are, by birth, banished ones, exiles, not from Eden merely, but from the God that made us.

Yet God has not forsaken us in the far country of our banishment. He has devised means whereby His banished be not expelled from him (2 Sam. 14:14). He pities, nay, yearns over us. Distance has not made Him forget us, or cease to care for us. Nay, our exiled condition is one of the things that calls forth His compassion. The Father sees His prodigals in the land of famine. His eye follows them. They may have lost sight of Him, but not He of them. He sends out His *grace* in search of them. The Son of His bosom comes down in quest of them. He shrinks not from entering the place of exile. He becomes a banished man for them. He lives an exile's life; He endures an exile's shame; He dies an exile's death; He is buried in an exile's tomb. All for us, the outcasts, the exiles! He takes our place of banishment, that we may take His place in His Father's many mansions. He stoops to our place of shame, that we may rise to His place of honour and glory. All that kept us in banishment, and that made it needful for God to banish us, He takes upon Himself. And thus it becomes a righteous thing in God to repeal the sentence of exile, and readmit us to His favour and presence—to put us in the place of children—nay, even in *His* place who came to seek that which was lost. For 'He was made sin for us, who knew no sin, that we might be made the righteousness of God in him' (2 Cor. 5:21).

Have you, reader, consented to this exchange? Have you accepted this substitution? He urges the exchange. He entreats you to take Him as your substitute. Why should you refuse or hesitate? It is life and home, and the restored fatherhood of the God from whom you are banished, that He presses on you. Are you too rich, too full, too fond of earth, to prize or to heed such blessings? Then think of the eternal banishment which awaits. How will you endure that? A few years outside of Eden and away from God may seem nothing to you, but how will you bear the everlasting exile? The song, and the dance, and the jest, and the cup may have lulled you into ease, or cheated your soul into forgetfulness: but soon these charms shall cease to blind you. The gay vision shall vanish; the eternal desert shall compass you about; and you will find, that in that place of exile there is nought but 'weeping and wailing and gnashing of teeth.'

But we are not only in the place of exile; we are in the region of death. We are far from the tree of life. The grave lies before us, with its bones and dust and darkness. Is there, then, in us the hope of resurrection and of the better life when death shall be swallowed up in victory? Have we made sure of this blessed hope by believing on Him who died and rose again, and who has said, 'I am the resurrection and the life; he that believeth in me, though he were dead, yet shall he live: and whosoever liveth and believeth in me, shall never die' (John 11:25)? This is our *one* hope. Have we made *sure* of it? It is not a far-off uncertainty that is set before us. It is a near, a real, and a blessed certainty: yet *free*, altogether free: not to be purchased by efforts, and struggles, and penances, and prayers, but by believing on Him who was dead and is alive again. As the resurrection and the life the Father has revealed Him. As such He has proclaimed Himself. To whom? To the dead in sin. And that word 'whosoever,' which He so often uses, is enough to tell every weary sinner on this side of the second death, that there is *life* freely presented to him through this living One, so that no one may say, 'I must die forever, because the fountain of life did not contain enough for me.'

If, reader, you know this risen One as your resting place, and this promise of resurrection as your hope and joy, then live like a stranger and a pilgrim here. Let your desires overleap the grave. Never let this earth be to you better than the outside of Eden. It may seem fair; it may dazzle you; it may look like an abiding home and a pleasant rest; but it is still a waste; it is still the dwelling of your great enemy, and the place where he spreads his snares. Arise and depart; this is not your rest, for it is polluted. Realise daily the difference between that which is and that which shall be. Let your life be that of one who is looking for the appearing of Him with whom your better life is hid, and with whom you shall appear in glory.*

---

* Since the above was written, I have found a passing remark in Dr Chalmers' *Daily Scripture Readings*, confirmatory of the view regarding the tree of life suggested at the beginning of this chapter: 'It accords with my whole understanding of what is sacred, whether in Christian or general philosophy, to accept of such information as is here given of the influence of a particular food on the soul of man—once I am satisfied with the credentials on which the proposed revelation is based.' —*Posthumous Works*, Vol. I. p. 6.

II

The Monument

But Eden does not forthwith pass away. God does not blast it and sweep it off the earth as soon as Adam is taken out of it. This might have been man's way, for it is how he deals with what offends his eye; but it is not God's, patience and longsuffering mark all His doings: He loves to spare; He lingers over His handiwork, loath to destroy it even when vile.

Eden still stands, though man has left it. The temple does not crumble down the moment that the worshipper has departed. In all likelihood, Eden shared the blight that then began to fall; but longevity, like that of the first ages of men, belonged to it. It took centuries to wither; yet it did wither; it was not to stand forever. Then, when it had decayed, and was waxing old, ready to vanish away, the deluge came and swept it off the earth.[*]

---

[*] Thus Milton describes it. Speaking of the deluge, he says—

...... Then shall this mount

But why was it allowed to remain at all? Surely this was no piece of chance, no thing without a meaning or an end?

To be a monument of what sin had done.
There stood the happy spot where man had dwelt; his birthplace, his first home, where he had walked with God. In looking at it daily, as he wandered round the sacred enclosure which he dared not to enter, he was reminded of what he had lost, and how it had been lost. Sin had done it all. 'Had it not been for sin,' he might muse with himself, 'I might have still been there, still happy, and dwelling amid the brightness that seems even yet to linger yonder: but sin has made me homeless, sin has spoiled me of my heritage; each day I am reminded of the greatness of my loss, and each day humbled at the thought that my own sin is the cause.' Every cloud that rested over it, every trace of decay that appeared on it, every leaf that was seen to fall, or was drifted over the enclosure into the plain without, would be to man a memorial of what sin had done—done to himself, done to paradise. Thus sin was embittered, and Adam humbled.

To show what value God affixes to the material creation.
He had laid the blight upon it, but he seemed most unwilling to destroy it. It was his own handiwork. He had so lately looked upon it with delight, and pronounced it

---

Of Paradise by might of waves be moved
Out of his place, push'd by the horned flood,
With all his verdure spoil'd and trees adrift,
Down the great river to the opening gulf.

Paradise Lost, b. xi.

good; how shall he 'give it up,' and sweep it away? This is the expression of God's estimate for the material creation. It is no carnal thing, nor is contact with it debasing or polluting. The truth is, that if we will but look at things in the light in which God places them before us, we shall find that it is not man who has been defiled by his contact with matter, but that it is matter which has been defiled by its contact with man. It was not Eden that ruined Adam; it was Adam that ruined Eden. 'The creature was made subject to vanity, not willingly, but by reason of him who subjected it' (Rom. 8:20-22). Nay, more; God tells us of the earnest expectation of creation, of its groans and travailings, of its longing to be delivered from the bondage of corruption into the glorious liberty of the sons of God. The value which God sets upon creation must be far higher than that which many amongst us are accustomed to place upon it. He still rejoices over his handiworks; He still keeps them before His eye, purposing, ere long, to cleanse and restore them all, clothing them with far more than primeval beauty in the day of 'the restitution of all things, spoken of by all the holy prophets since the world began' (Acts 3:21).

To show that God had not forsaken the earth.
It was His own earth, His own dwelling. Here He had pitched His tent, and reared His palace. Sin has made Him stand aloof from these, for a season; but He still preserves them in being—though sorely marred—to intimate that He has not abandoned them; nay, that He means to return

and dwell there, as of old. Look at Eden, or at paradise its fair garden within; it is but the ruins of His former dwelling, the relics of His temple. Yet why are these ruins so carefully enclosed and protected? Why are they left thus in half decay? Why care for them so watchfully? Why not allow man to trample on them, or the storm to waste them, or the earthquake to swallow them up? To show that He had a purpose respecting them, of which purpose they were to be a visible pledge to man. A voice came out from these guarded 'walks and bowers,' proclaiming, 'I have not utterly forsaken the earth, nor the place which I had chosen to put my name there, nor yet the spirits which I have made.' And was not this the voice of *grace*?— grace that mourned over the ruin which sin had made, yet refused to give way to sin, or to allow it utterly to trample down so goodly a creation, by driving out the God that made it, from His dwelling there?

To show that man shall yet return and possess the material creation.

God did not mean to mock man by preserving Eden and keeping him within sight of it. He wished to teach him something of His gracious purpose, not only regarding His deliverance from the enemy, but also regarding the inheritance provided for him. Therefore God kept Eden in view, as a type of the coming inheritance, on which man shall enter when all things are made new, and he has passed through death to the glory of the resurrection-life, over which death shall have no power. God was thus saying to man: 'There Eden stands, ruined and faded; yet to it you will one day return. Behold the pledge! There shall be a better Eden—an Eden passing through decay to restitution, as you are to pass through death to resurrection—"a new heavens and a new earth, wherein dwelleth righteousness."' One, in our own day, has been thought to utter deep truth when he said—

> 'Earth can never meet the heaven,
> Never can the there be here.'—Schiller.

Yet it is not so. He was uttering but the world's wisdom; he knew not God's purpose when he thus spoke. Heaven and earth are yet to meet: the *there* shall yet be *here*.

What lessons of *grace* were here! On how many objects and scenes did God write these lessons, that man might read them everywhere, and learn the fulness of that reconciliation which God was making known to him, and the surpassing glory as well as blessedness which God was keeping in reserve for him! Well might He call Himself 'the God of all grace;' and well might He swear by Himself, 'As I live, saith the Lord, I have no pleasure in the death of the sinner.' The God who could so affectionately care for the guilty and the hateful, and who could be at such pains to exhibit His care in ways so manifold, in order that man might not misread or mistake His meaning, must be the same God as He who said, 'Let the wicked forsake his ways, and the unrighteous man his thoughts, and let him return to the Lord, for he will have mercy on him, and to our God, for he will abundantly pardon.'

Are we then reading *grace* in each object around? Do we see the infinite grace implied in our being kept, even for one day, out of the place of woe? Are we gathering up new lessons of grace from every leaf fall as well as from every bud, from each blade of grass, and each drop of dew? Are all these to us messages of grace from a redeeming God? Do we use them to quiet our rising doubts, to reassure our drooping souls? Is He who gives the temporal not far more willing to give the spiritual? Will He who feeds our bodies famish our souls?

And do not all these things point forward to the wondrous future? Do they not speak of 'the grace that is to be brought to us at the revelation of Jesus Christ'? (1 Pet. 1:13). Do they not with one voice foretell the 'ages to come,' when God is 'to show the *exceeding riches of his grace* in his kindness towards us through Christ Jesus' (Eph. 2:7)?

Yet that future has a dark side too. There is infinite grace to be then brought out to view, but this is only for those who have believed it here and have fled to this gracious God in this the 'day of grace.' Their glory and their joy shall know no bounds. But as to the world—the dark, the blinded world—what awaits them? Not grace: they have spurned it. Not life: they have chosen death. Not 'the world to come:' they have preferred this 'present evil world.' And as they have sowed, so shall they reap forever. The 'wrath of God abideth upon them.' To them 'the mist of darkness is reserved forever.' The curse shall burst upon them like a thunder-cloud and continue throughout the ages to come to discharge its fierceness upon their heads.

Poor world! Is this the end of your brief day of mirth?—the end of all hope, the beginning of all despair? Your feasts are over; your gay-lighted halls of midnight are dark! The noise of the viol has ceased; lust is quenched, and revelry is dumb; beauty, and rank, and splendour, have vanished like a dream. The trumpet summons you, but it is not to festival; it is to the judgment seat! Oh! what a reckoning awaits you there! And after the reckoning, what a sentence! It invites you to no open paradise, but consigns you to the second death; it writes no 'new name' upon your forehead, nor seals you among the bleat: it puts into your hands a scroll whereon is written, within and without, in letters of fire, 'Lamentation, and mourning, and woe.'*

---

*   I know not if such warnings were ever clothed in words of greater power than the following:—

> The gay glory of time shall depart, and sportful liberty shall be bound forever in the chain of obdurate necessity. The green earth, with all her blooming beauty and bowers of peace, shall depart. The morning and evening salutations of kinsmen shall depart; and the ever welcome voice of friendship, and the tender whispering of full hearted affection, shall depart, for the sad discord of weeping and wailing and gnashing of teeth; and the tender names of children, and father and mother, and wife and husband, with the communion of domestic love and mutual affection, and the inward touches of natural instinct, which family compact, when uninvaded by discord, wraps the live-long day into one swell of tender emotion, making earth's lowly scenes to breathe of heaven itself;—all, all shall pass away, and instead shall come the level lake that burns, and the solitary dungeon, and the desolate bosom, and the throes and tossings of horror and hopelessness, and the worm that dies not, and the fire that is not quenched.

Over the blight of Eden we may grieve. For the wreck of this fair world we may take up a lamentation. But for these our grief need not be long or sore. Tears for these, however natural, may soon be dried; for they fade only to reflourish in fresher beauty. But over the blight of human joys, the wreck of undying souls, we may well weep as those who have no hope. The lost are lost forever. They pass away, and return not. The second death yields back no victims ; the lake of fire allows no brand be plucked from its everlasting burnings.

'Tis written, 'tis written, 'tis sealed of heaven, and a few years shall reveal it all. Be assured, it is even so to happen to the despisers of holy writ. With this in arrear, what boots liberty, pleasure, enjoyment—all within the hour-glass of time, or the round of earth's continent, all the sensibilities of life, all the powers of man, all the attractions of woman?

12

THE GUARD

Now that the worshipper has gone out, the gates of the temple are closed. He is not permitted to re-enter, nor is any other foot to tread the forsaken courts, or any other voice to offer worship there. The shrine is to stand in loneliness, unentered, untrodden, more desolate in its ruined splendour than Petra, or Palmyra, or Persepolis, in after-years.

All access was barred. God Himself did this. Yet not by the mere issuing of a command, for Adam could not again be trusted with that, but by placing 'a flaming sword, which turned every way, to keep the way of the tree of life.' Such were the precautions taken by God to prevent re-entrance. They were precautions of the most striking kind. A sword, nay, a sword of flame, turning every way, so as to face and arrest every intruder. This was the guard set by God to mark what importance He attached to man's expulsion and exclusion.

The thought may have, perhaps, occurred—'Why not uproot the tree of life at once?' This seems the simplest way of preventing man from touching it; but God had a purpose to serve by allowing that tree to remain. He meant to teach man that there was still a tree of life, though it was to be hidden from his eye, or, at least, placed beyond his reach. That tree he should one day revisit, and of its fruit he should yet be given to eat; but now it was inaccessible, and death would be the penalty of attempting to force an approach to it.

It was thus distinctly intimated that there was a hindrance in the way of man's re-entering Eden, and partaking of the tree of life. That hindrance must be removed, and towards its removal God was now to *direct His efforts*, if we may so express it. Yet, till it should be removed, and that in a righteous way, man must remain without. That hindrance was *sin*, or rather, the righteous law, which alone gave to sin its obstructing power; for 'the strength of sin is the law.'

The visible hindrance was a flaming sword; that is to say, it was more than a mere fence cast across the way, or a closing of the gate against the sinner. It not only prohibited entrance, but it announced to man that if he endeavoured to enter he should certainly perish—perish under the stroke of Him who is a consuming fire. The *old* way of access was thus shut up, nay, guarded by the sword of the fiery law—the inexorable law, that would abate no jot or tittle of its righteous claims. And woe be to him who should attempt to enter through this guarded way! Such an attempt would not merely be fruitless, but it would be avenged with death, a death which would be but the beginning of the 'everlasting burnings.' God in His own time would open a 'new and living way;' but, meanwhile, entrance was denied. Man must stand afar off. His former nearness to God is for a time denied.

This flaming sword evidently corresponded to the veil in the temple, which shut out Israel from the Holy of Holies. Paradise was the innermost part of Eden. There God had dwelt, there he had planted the tree of life, there was his presence chamber. It thus resembled the Holy of Holies, which occupied the interior shrine of the temple; and Eden itself would represent the Holy Place, or second court. Outside of this again, and in front of the gate of Eden, would be placed the altar whereon Adam laid his sacrifice, answering to the Outer Court, where the brazen altar stood.

Whether the flaming sword waved before Eden, or merely before Paradise, we are not expressly told. Only we may be led to suppose the latter, from its being said that its object was to guard the way to the tree of life, which was in Paradise, the farthest and most eastern recess of Eden. If this be the case, it answers still more closely to the veil of the temple, which was drawn before the entrance into the holiest of all.

The sword and the veil, then, served the same end. They were meant to teach man that there did exist a hindrance in the way of his return to the presence of God, or, as the apostle states it, 'the Holy Ghost thus signified that the way into the holiest of all was not yet made manifest' (Heb. 9:8). There was a mighty difficulty to be overcome; sin must be atoned for, a sacrifice must be provided, and this must be no common victim. The fiery law must be appeased and removed out of the way. All this could only be done at an infinite cost: it must, moreover, occupy a long period of time; it must be a work of stupendous labour. And, meanwhile, till it was accomplished, the holiest must be shut up—there must be distance between God and man.

In this way, not only was the awful lesson taught of what sin had done, and how much its undoing was to cost, but time was afforded for fully unfolding the real nature of sin, God's estimate of it, as well as the manner in which it was to be taken out of the way. For this end, sacrifice was forthwith instituted. God taught man to bring his burnt offering to the gate of Eden, in front of the flaming sword, and lay it upon the altar there. Thus man learnt that 'without the shedding of blood there was no remission of sin.' He learnt also that it was by means of blood that the sword was to be withdrawn, its flame quenched, and the way reopened for the sinner, or, rather, 'a new and living way consecrated for us,' right through this veil—this sword of fire.

Man thus saw that salvation was wholly of God, not of or from himself. He had done the evil, but God only could undo it. He had opened the flood gate; God only could close it. The hindrance was one which could be removed only by God. He placed the flaming sword there, and He only could withdraw it; He had barred up paradise, He alone could unbar it. Not man's efforts, or prayers, or tears, or blood, but God alone, could open up the way. 'He openeth, and no man can shut; he shutteth, and no man can open.'

And there lay the sacrifice, bleeding in front of the flaming sword—telling of Him who is the just God, yet the Saviour; the avenger of sin, yet the redeemer of the sinner. There lay the sacrifice, which fire from the flaming sword was consuming, sending up its smoke, as if wrestling with some mighty adversary, and striving to quench the flame that forbade the sinner's access. There lay the sacrifice, as if knocking at the closed gate of paradise for man, and pleading for his readmission, offering to bear his sin and pay his penalty. And each new victim laid upon the altar was a new knock at that awful gate, a new cry of intercession lifted up on man's behalf.

During four thousand years that cry continued ascending from many altars. Yet the gate opened not. The sword still waved; the veil still shut out the holiest from man. For 'it was not possible that the blood of bulls and goats could take away sin' (Heb. 10:4). A nobler sacrifice was needed, and richer blood must flow.

At length the flame went out, the sword departed, the 'veil was rent in twain from the top to the bottom.' The better sacrifice had been found, towards which all the others pointed forward. The better blood had been shed, the blood of the Lamb of God, 'the Lamb without blemish and without spot, who verily was foreordained before the foundation of the world, but was manifested in these last times for us' (1 Pet. 1:19). The only begotten of the Father, the eternal Son, had taken flesh, and laid Himself upon the altar to bear the stroke and receive the fire into His own bosom. God spoke and said, 'Awake, O sword, against the man that is my fellow' (Zech. 13:7). The sword awoke. It smote with fiery edge this divine sacrifice, but, in so doing, it was quenched. The blood which it drew forth from the victim quenched the flame. The hindrance of four thousand years was now removed, and the way into the holiest thrown open to the sinner. Man needs no longer to stand without.

That way stands still open. The sword has not returned to its place, nor the veil been mended or restored. Nay, more, that way has been sprinkled with blood, and made safe for a sinner to tread upon. Nay, more still, that inner sanctuary has been also sprinkled with blood, so that a sinner may go in and worship there with safety to himself, and without defiling the sacred floor and walls. Nay, more still, there is a mercy-seat within, a throne of *grace*; and on that mercy-seat the Son of God is sitting—Jesus of Nazareth, the woman's seed, the conqueror, the man with the bruised heel, our kinsman, our brother, who took flesh for us. 'He has led captivity captive; he has received gifts for men, even for the rebellious, that the Lord God might dwell among them.'

What more can any sinner need to assure him of a welcome? Are we satisfied that the sword is removed, and the veil rent? Then let us go in. Are we satisfied that the way has been opened, and the blood sprinkled, so as to make it safe for us to enter? Then let us go in. Are we satisfied that there is a mercy-seat, that Jesus is there, and that He has done enough to secure our acceptance? Then, though the chief of sinners, let us go in. 'Let us come boldly to the throne of grace, that we may obtain mercy and find grace to help in time of need.' 'Having boldness [that is, liberty to come without fear or doubt] to enter into the holiest by the blood of Jesus, by a new and living way which he hath consecrated for us, through the veil, that is to say, his flesh; and having an high priest over the house of God ; let us draw near with a true heart, in full assurance of faith, having our hearts sprinkled from an evil conscience, and our bodies washed with pure water' (Heb. 10:19-22).

'But am I to go in just as I am?' Yes. In what other way do you propose to go? Are all these gracious preparations which God has made, by the sprinkling of the blood and the erection of a mercy-seat, not enough? And, if not enough, what would you add to them? When the Holy Spirit opens your eye to see the warrant of entrance, does He reveal something new to you, something not contained in what the Son of God has done? Or is not His object and His office to show you that finished work as the only thing that can embolden you to come, and the free message of divine love as your only warrant? Nay, and is it not His aim to keep you from seeking any other ground of boldness, any other warrant, any other plea, any other recommendation, either within or without, either in heaven or earth? Does He not open your eyes to see that the work of Christ takes for granted that you are just what you are, and nothing else? And that, if there is not enough to invite you in just as you are, your case must be forever hopeless, unless there should come a second Saviour to complete what you seem to suppose the first has left undone?

'But my sins! They are crimson. They rise mountain high.' Yes, it is even so. They are ten thousand times worse than you imagine them. But shall this bar your entrance? For whom was that mercy-seat erected? For those who could plead fewest sins—sins less dark than others? No. That you will not say. The number of your sins, the blackness of your guilt, only makes it the more suitable for you, and ought to lead you to prize it the more.

'But a soul, guilty like mine, would defile that holy place. These feet would stain its pure pavement—this breath would pollute its air.' Nay, but look. See that blood that is sprinkled on its floor and walls. That makes them impervious to defilement. The guiltiest sinner may come in, and still there will be no defilement so long as that blood is there. It cannot be to cleanse that sanctuary that the blood thus lies upon it. The place is holy. It must be to prevent defilement from the sinner who enters. And this it does completely. Were you far viler than you are, you need not fear. Even *you* cannot defile it. The sprinkled blood has made that an impossibility.

'But will it not dishonour God to admit and welcome such as I am?' Nay, it will not. He has provided for that. He has made it a righteous thing to receive you; and how can that which is righteous dishonour Him? But more than this. The only way in which He can get glory from you is just by your coming and being forgiven. You cannot glorify Him in any other way. You are shut up to this. Your refusal to come dishonours Him; but your coming honours Him. What strange, yet what blessed tidings, we bring you, when we tell you that the only way left for you to glorify God is by coming at once to him and being received into his family as a son!

'But my hard and stony heart, so insensible, so impenitent!—how can I venture in with it as it is?' What! And is not He who sits upon the mercy-seat exalted a Prince and a Saviour to *give repentance*? How can you then think of standing without? Besides, what will *waiting* do for you? Will remaining outside soften your heart or produce repentance? You know it will not. So that if there be peril and presumption in venturing in, there is far more of these in standing without.

Will you not then at once go in? All things are ready. The sword no longer guards the way. Paradise—paradise lost is again thrown open to you. The sanctuary of God, with its unfolded gate, stands ready to receive you. A rent veil, a consecrated way, a sprinkled mercy-seat, a gracious high priest—all these, with one voice, beckon you in without delay. And are the wastes of earth better than the bowers of paradise, or the house of your God?

And see the symbols of redemption already set up in paradise, as they were afterwards in the temple. See the cherubim far within, yet not out of sight. They are the types of ransomed men, visible pledges of a redeemed creation. Adam, looking at them, would read in them the assurance of his own entrance upon the inheritance, in due time. They told him that he was one day again to be where they now were. They were placed on the very spot where he had lately been; and thus they announced to him the certainty of his re-entrance, when the hindrances were removed and the flaming sword withdrawn.*

And would not that bright symbol draw the eye of Adam, and awaken in his heart unutterable longings after the inheritance? It would make him weary to be there; and earnestly to desire the time when paradise should be restored to him and he to paradise. 'How long, O Lord?' would be the burden of his daily prayers. 'Come quickly, thou seed of the woman, thou opener of the gates of Eden, thou conqueror of the serpent and of the serpent's seed.' It would give him more truly to feel as a stranger and a pilgrim—one who was weary of earth and sin, and who was 'hasting to the coming of the day of God,' when all

---

*   I take for granted here that the cherubim are the symbols of redemption— the figures of the redeemed. This seems now very generally conceded. For, from the beginning to the end of Scripture, they are always seen in connexion with redemption. They occupy the innermost part of Eden, just as they occupied the holiest in the temple. These, of course, were figures; but the reality is given us in the Apocalypse, when they sing, 'Thou hast redeemed us by thy blood out of every kindred and nation,' (Rev. 5:9), etc. Our notions on many of these points are much at fault. We hear and read in many an author of the 'wings of angels,' of 'angelic harps and crowns,' etc. Scripture never speaks thus. No. The wing, the crown, the harp, the palm, belong to the redeemed alone. In the passage in Genesis, the cherubim are not holding or wielding the flaming sword. They are there for a very different end; to be a visible pledge of man's re-entrance into, and re-occupation of, Eden.

things should be made new, and the evil which he had brought into the world undone forever.

Reader, and especially young reader, will you now take one closing message? I speak to those who are still aliens from God. It is a hard and thankless task to which you are setting yourself—to build for yourself a home in the wilderness, where you may enjoy life while it lasts, and forget the bleak wastes that surround you. There is no peace for your soul in scenes where God is not. Apart from Him, life is not life, but utter death—nay, the very death of deaths. Out of Him all joy is madness, and in the midst of it the heart is oppressed and unsatisfied. Your very being seems withered and hollow, even when mirth is flushing the cheek, and fond visions of earthly gaiety are luring you onward. For none of these can heal your hidden wound. They cannot quench your soul's thirst or fill its ever-craving void. They soothe no sorrow, they dry up no tears, they knit no broken bonds. They assuage not pain, nor calm the throbbing pulse, nor fence you from disease, nor charm away death, nor light up the tomb. In spite of them, the last trumpet shall sound; and you shall hear it, whether in the grave or in the midst of your revelry. And what will pleasure avail you in that day?

Will you still madly chase these dreams when the end is so certain and so terrible? Will you not leave a world that never satisfied you, and which is so soon to pass away? Will you not quench your thirst at the well of living water? For is it not said, 'Let him that is athirst come'? There is an open paradise and a tree of life, to which no flaming sword denies you access; will you not, then, go boldly in? What can make you hesitate? Earth and hell cannot hinder; God invites; His Word bids you welcome; enter in.

You have heard the wondrous story of the grace of God. It is grace such as would cover all your sins, soothe all your troubles, and gladden you with an infinite joy. It is grace that would provide you with a rich portion here, and a far richer inheritance hereafter. Will you not then retrace your steps, and seek a home in that bosom whence all that grace is flowing?*

It will be a home for eternity, from which you shall go out no more.

---

* The following striking extract from a German writer may help to enforce the sentiment above dwelt upon:—

> I was a spectator a short time since of a gay assembly at N—, some ranging themselves for the dance, others at the card-tables, and numbers attracting notice by their personal decorations. I looked on the motley throng with a tear of thankfulness that I knew something better. At times I felt such compassion for the poor deluded beings, that I was ready to cry aloud among them, 'Seek what ye seek; but it is not where ye seek.' For what were they all seek? Lasting enjoyment. What did they find? Fleeting enjoyment with lasting pain. The dancing, especially, seemed to me a sad and affecting emblem of human life. I watched, in imagination, those engaged in it. They approach, divide, pass and repass each other, and under the constant excitement of the music prolong the diversion, overwhelmed with heat and dust, till it ends in complete exhaustion. And when, after all the coming and going, joining in the dance, or resting, the day dawns, and the hall is gradually emptied of the jaded crowd, how forcibly are we reminded of the termination of a life squandered in vanity! The dim and sinking lights show here and there, through the dusty atmosphere, a torn riband, or the lost badge of an order, lying on the floor, the only traces of the recent occupants. —THOLUCK'S *Guido and Julius*, p. 199.

13

THE TWO WORSHIPPERS

Henceforth, all worship must be carried on outside of Eden; for that sacred enclosure is now forbidden ground. Intercourse between God and man is not to cease; but it is restricted. The close intimacy of the unfallen state—in which there was no veil, no distance, no interposing medium of communication—is at an end.

God still permits, nay, commands man, the sinner, to draw near and hold fellowship; but he must stand without. It is only the outer court which the worshipper is at liberty to use. All within this is carefully fenced off from his intrusion. He may take his place close to the guarded entrance; he may build his altar under the very gleam of the flaming sword; he may pitch his tent within full sight of the cherubim: but not one step farther, even for worship, is he permitted to take.

Yet permission to worship, in any circumstance and under any restriction, is a declaration of *grace* on the part of God. Liberty to approach and converse, indicated most distinctly to man the gracious purpose of the divine mind which was now beginning to open. Nothing but free love in God could lead Him still to acknowledge man as a worshipper, and to accept his worship. It mattered not that there were shadows and distance between. The existence of these was not incompatible with grace. For, simply to be recognised as one who, though a sinner, is yet at liberty to come to God and commune with Him on any spot of earth, however far from Eden, is as distinct an assurance of grace as could be given. Nor could Adam fail to understand it as such. Whatever might be the restrictions as to the place and the manner of approach, still, so long as he was at liberty 'to come before the Lord and to bow himself before the High God' as a welcome and accepted worshipper, he could not but see that 'there was forgiveness with God that he might be feared' (Ps. 130:4).

The method and the medium of communication were, no doubt, new and strange. It was only with blood in his hand that man could draw near. In no other way would God deal with him. But this indicated no reluctance to receive the sinner. It was no withdrawal of grace, nor did it intimate a desire to throw hindrances in the way of the worshipper. Neither did it imply any uncertainty in man's warrant to approach; nor encourage anything like doubtfulness on his part respecting his welcome from God, as if grace was hung upon conditions whose fulfilment was still a matter of suspense. Rather the opposite. For while God was pointing man's eye to obstacles of the most formidable kind, He was declaring, at the same time, His willingness to have them all removed; nay, the absolute certainty of His purpose not to rest till they were entirely surmounted, whatever might be the cost, the time, the toil required in the accomplishment of the stupendous work.

Thus Adam worshipped, with Eve, 'the mother of all living,'—the mother of the promised seed. And the Being whom he worshipped outside of Eden, was the same Jehovah with whom he had communed within its blessed shades; only it was now as the God of *grace* that he approached Him. Day by day did he lay his lamb upon the altar in token of his belief that it was only *grace* that had kept him from the same consuming fire that was devouring his offering; and also that it was through that blood alone that even grace could reach him and the God of grace accept him.

But time went on, and Adam stood no longer alone at the altar. The children whom God had given him came with him. From their earliest years he had doubtless brought them to that place of sacrifice and instructed them as to its design. They knelt along with him upon the turf, while he praised and confessed and made supplication to the Lord, as the smoke of the burnt offering went up to heaven or fell in wreaths over the trees of Eden. There seemed to be but 'one lip' and one heart, even as there was but one family and one altar. This, however, was not to continue long. The children grew up, and a strange difference began to manifest itself. Hitherto there had seemed to be but one worshipper; now there were two, and these at entire variance with each other, as if there were two Gods, diverse in character, to whom they were paying their homage. Let us look at these two worshippers and mark the difference between them. It is evidently on no minor point that they differ, and that the views which they entertain, both of God's character and their own, are opposed to each other as noon is to midnight. Nay, it seems to be a different God that they are worshipping.

One thing strikes us much in this narrative respecting Cain and Abel. In them the two great divisions of Adam's race begin to show themselves: the seed of the woman and the seed of the serpent. Very quickly, indeed, has this separation taken place. It arises in the first generation, in the first family. The first man born of a woman is a child of the devil, one of the serpent's brood. This difference is not between two neighbours, or friends, or distant kinsmen, but between two brothers; born of one mother—of that very woman to whom the promise was made; born within sight of Eden, and with no example of abounding iniquity to mislead and corrupt. This difference is not one of birth. By nature they are the same, begotten in the likeness of their fallen father; not like him, in the image of God. In Abel, however, we see a monument of divine power, a specimen of the Holy Spirit's work, a trophy of Jehovah's sovereign choice. It is not the firstborn, but the younger, that is chosen; 'the last is first, and the first last.' 'Even so, Father, for so it seemed good in thy sight.'

Nor are these two brothers without some points of resemblance even in the things of God. They both profess to acknowledge the same God. They both come to worship Him. They bring gifts in their hands. They come to the same altar. They observe the same time and place of worship. In these respects, they are the same. But there the likeness ends and the difference begins.

In the opinion of the world, these outward features of resemblance are far greater and more important than the points of contrast. Man, in setting up his religion, looks only at the outward and the visible. If he gets these, he asks no more; nay, he thinks that God has no right to expect more.

> ... Mouth honour, breath,
> Which the poor heart would fain deny,
>   but dare not.[*]

This is what passes with him under the name of religion! A few prayers and alms deeds, a reputable life, church attending decency, 'reception of the sacrament'—these are the essential items in the world's religion. But all these items are to be found in Cain's religion, too. The two, indeed, are identical. And if God rejected the worship of the latter, will he accept that of the former? Is the first Cain to be cast off, and his offspring acknowledged and welcomed? No. God sees not as man sees: nor does He take the test of earthly balances, which can only weigh the visible and the external. He uses the balances of the sanctuary. And 'the things which are highly esteemed among men are

---

[*]   Shakespeare, *Macbeth*, 5.3.29-30.

abomination in the sight of God.' Man's religion has no more resemblance to God's religion, than have the sands of the desert to the groves of Eden. But let us mark more minutely the difference between the two worshippers.

First, Abel comes as a sinner, as one who had naturally no right to come, and who could present no claim for acceptance arising from anything about himself. Cain comes simply as a creature, as one who had a right to approach the God that made him. There is no acknowledgment of sin upon his lips or in his hand. He knew how his father had come before he fell, and he is resolved to come in that very way again. Confession of sin he will not stoop to. His desert of wrath he will not own. Yet still he comes to God. He does not think this unnecessary. Nay, perhaps he thinks it right and seemly. He must have a religion—but the 'religion of nature' is all that he will consent to. A recognition of God as creator, and of himself as creature, he is willing to make; but no more. God's right to homage he admits; and he feels, perchance, a pride, it may be a pleasure, in rendering that homage. The favour of God he sees to be desirable, and he is willing to part with some of his substance to purchase it. But he will not stoop to confess that he has done anything to forfeit that favour. He will not approach God as one who has deservedly lost it. If God will receive him as a creature, and his gifts as thank-offerings for favours bestowed, he will come; for by these gifts he thinks to keep himself from being wholly a debtor to God. But he will not come, save in some such way.

In a very different way does Abel draw near. He feels that it is only as a sinner that he can come; and that it is only in that character that God can deal with him, or he with God. He does not hide nor palliate his guilt. He does not cast the blame upon others, nor upon his own circumstances, as if he could not help sinning. He does not accuse the law of being too strict, or the lawgiver of being too severe. He comes as a sinner, laying the guilt on no one but himself. The Holy Spirit has taught him what sin is, so that he has learnt to abhor himself because of it. Yet that same Spirit has taught him that God 'receiveth sinners,' who come to him *as such*. And therefore he comes. All that he knows about himself is that he is a sinner; yet, having 'known and believed' that story of grace which God taught his father when he sinned, he does not stand afar off, but draws near at once, attracted and emboldened by the grace which that story reveals. That grace he sees to be as sufficient as it is suitable. This is his encouragement and his confidence. He comes, because the God of grace has invited him to do so. Does he need more than this? However evil he may be, the grace that is in God tells him that he is welcome.

Second, Abel comes acknowledging death to be his due; for he lays his bleeding lamb upon the altar. Cain will not own this and brings but the fruit of his garden as his gift. There is nothing that betokens death in that which he brings; for he denies that death is his due. Possibly his offering might be as valuable in itself as Abel's. It would cost more toil; for it was gotten by the sweat of his brow in tilling the ground. Yet there was no death acknowledged in it; and therefore no acceptance either for his gift or for himself. For so long as death was not acknowledged as the wages of sin, grace could not flow out. Grace takes for granted the infinite evil of sin, and that nothing short of death is its due. With the man that will not own this, grace refuses to deal. He may own that he is a sinner; but unless he owns that he is such a sinner as is totally unworthy of life, grace turns away. Not that there is not grace enough even for him; but he is shutting it out: he is doing that thing which would make it dishonouring to God to extend it to him; he is putting himself in a position, and taking to himself a character, in which grace cannot recognise him.

It was as one deserving of death that Abel came, as one who felt himself under the sentence, 'The soul that sinneth, it shall die.' He brought with him the visible symbol of this, in the lamb which he laid upon the altar. Thus he was saying each time he brought it, 'I deserve to die; for death is the wages of sin—nothing less than death; either I must die, or another must die for me: if I die, then I am shut out forever from God, for the dead cannot praise him; if another dies for me, then it is just as if I had died and borne the curse myself; in that case I am set free, and allowed to come to God as if the whole penalty had been paid, or had never been due. Let this death, then, which I bring, stand for my death, and let that curse, which was my due, pass over to this substitute.' Thus it was that Abel took God's estimate of sin and its penalty; and thus it was that he took God's method of atoning for that sin and paying that penalty. His conscience was pacified; his soul found rest in God. He saw that this death was the channel through which grace was flowing to the sinner, and that it was by taking his place as one whose desert was death, that grace was to flow to himself.

Is this the place that we are taking, the footing upon which we are seeking to stand before God? No other will avail us. A less humbling one may suit our pride and self-righteousness, but it will secure only rejection from God. It is to this that the Holy Spirit is seeking to bring us, when he 'convinces of sin.' For it is thus that he shows us what sin is, and what are its wages. It is thus that he brings us to the experience of him that said, 'I acknowledged my sin unto thee, and mine iniquity have I not hid. I said, I will confess my transgressions unto the Lord; *and thou forgavest the iniquity of my sin.*' (Ps. 32:5).

Third, Abel comes with the blood in his hand. There is no blood seen on Cain. Perhaps he thought it unnatural as well as unnecessary. He might point to the stream of blood from Abel's lamb, and contrast it with the beauty of his own fruit offering which no blood disfigured. He might scornfully contrast the struggles of the suffering lamb with his painless and more attractive offering. He might, perchance, like many a modern pretender to reason, thank God that his was not a religion of blood, whatever his brother's might be. He, at least, was not adding to creation's sorrow! His religion was too rational, too pure, to admit of that! It had nothing to do with the destruction of God's creatures!

Yet it was just the want of that blood that was the cause of his rejection. Whatever man may say, yet God will accept nothing which the blood has not consecrated. It would be defilement to do so. The blood is the only thing that can fit a sinner for going near God. 'Without shedding of blood there is no remission.' That blood can cleanse even a Cain, and secure his acceptance, if he will but make use of it. But if he undervalue it, if he trample on it, then rejection must be his doom. The blood that would have cleansed him, will condemn him forever.

Abel took the blood and stood before God on the spot where it was flowing. The Holy Spirit had taught him its meaning. It is the blood that gives him peace, that cleanses, that heals, that emboldens him to come to God, without a sense of guilt upon his soul. It is the blood that purges his conscience from dead works to serve the living God; for it is this that tells him of wrath laid on a substitute and forever passed away from himself.* He sees that this is God's way of saving him; and he is content with it. He desires no other. He finds the stream of free love pouring itself along this crimson channel, and he pitches his tent upon its banks. He asks no other dwelling save that, beside which this 'river of God' is flowing.

---

*   Perhaps some of our readers may here call to mind the well-known hymn which thus begins:—

> I will praise thee every day,
> Now thine anger's turn'd away:
> Comfortable thoughts arise
> From the bleeding sacrifice.

Fourth, Abel comes resting on the promise—the promise which made known the riches of divine grace, and invited the sinner to draw near. He could not venture without a promise; but that which God had given was enough. It revealed enough of God to quiet every fear. Had it not been for that promise he could not have come; nay, he would have fled away: but with words of grace such as these, he can come 'with boldness;' he can 'draw near with a true heart, and in the full assurance of faith.' Viewing that promise in connexion with the sacrifice on his altar, he gets a glimpse of the coming deliverer, and of the love which He is to bring fully into view. His eye passes along the ages till it rests on the true seed of the woman, the better sacrifice. He recognises the bruised heel; and in it the conqueror of Satan. In the promise he discerns the grace; in the sacrifice, the way in which the dispensing of that grace becomes an act of righteousness. And keeping his eye on these two things thus placed side by side, he is confident before God, and can lift up trustful hands, even to the Holy One who hates iniquity.

To Cain the promise is nought. He acts as one that needs no promise and no grace. He comes without any thought of an invitation; nay, such a thing is an incumbrance in his estimation, for it takes for granted what he is by no means willing to admit, that he needs a promise and must be a debtor to grace alone. He acts as if he could invite himself; nay, as if he could be his own saviour; or, rather, as if he did not need a saviour at all.

What is this promise in *our* eyes? What is the value *we* put upon it? Do we see it as that in which the free love of God is wrapped up, and on which it is inscribed in glowing characters? Is it this that attracts us, that assures us, that gladdens us? Does it rebuke all fear and awaken all confidence? Is it to us like the Lord's own gracious voice, 'Come unto me and I will give you rest'—'Him that cometh unto me I will in no wise cast out'? Is this the staff on which we lean, as we pass in through the veil into the holiest?

What, then, was the *chief* difference between these two brothers? It was just this. The one believed the story of grace, and the other disbelieved it. We have seen several shades of difference, but they all involve this. Abel's whole religion rested upon this grace, and not one of his religious acts has any meaning apart from this. Cain's religion was totally unconnected with grace; nay, it denied it, and proceeded independently of it. Such was the chief feature of difference. It seems a small one; yet in God's sight it was everything. It was simply on account of this, that the one was cast off and the other welcomed as a beloved son.

It was the same story of grace which was made known to both. The same parental lips had told it, the same scenes had announced it. There was no difference in the grace or in the mode of telling it. Both brothers had heard the tale of love; perhaps too from God Himself: for it is plain, from what follows in the narrative, that Cain was no stranger to the voice of God. Yet the one brother listens to it and welcomes it, the other closes his ear against it and turns away. It was the belief of this story that made Abel what he was—a child of God; it was Cain's unbelief that made God reject both his offering and himself.

There is the same division still among the children of men. At the head of the one class is seen 'righteous Abel;' at the head of the other is Cain the murderer. The one class consists of those who, believing this story of grace as now made known so fully in the cross of the Lord Jesus Christ, have gone to God and taken their joyful place among His sons, living meanwhile the life of pilgrims and strangers here. The other is made up of those who, not believing this story, nor heeding the cross, nor prizing the blood, are still remaining aliens, nay, fugitives—men without a portion here, or an inheritance hereafter.

Are we living Abel's life of faith? Is the blood of the sacrifice that which speaks to us the 'better things,' so that each misgiving of our troubled hearts forthwith passes off, when it appears, like mist before the risen sun? Is the sight of that blood all we need to call us back to peace, when sin or doubt has come between us and God? Is the knowledge of its infinite value enough to give us at all times the complete assurance that there is no sin of ours, however great, which it cannot at once wash away, so that, 'being once purged, we have no more conscience of sin'? (Heb. 10:2). Does one look at that blood reassure our hearts when the cloud of guilt spreads darkly over us? And does that one look comfort us unspeakably more than the whole sum of our evidences, the whole register of our graces? Does it so entirely satisfy us, as that while on the one hand it makes us no longer afraid to look down into the depths of our guilt, so on the other it frees us from every wish to know ourselves, or to be known of God, as anything but the 'chief of sinners'? Does the security, which that blood is designed to give us, of acceptance with God, appear to us so certain and so strong, that, with nothing else to recommend us or answer for us, but the blood alone, we can go to God as trustfully and simply as Adam did, ere sin had broken his confidence and cast him out from the presence of the Lord?

As those on whom this blood is sprinkled, are we separating ourselves from a present evil world, feeling that this blood, in removing the veil which hung between us and God, has done so, only to draw it between us and the world? We look *before* us, to the place where Jehovah is, and, behold, the veil has vanished! God and we have come together, face to face, meeting in peace and communing in love. But we cast our eye *behind* us, to the 'tents of wickedness,' where we dwelt so long—and, lo, the veil has come between them and us! We feel that, just as formerly it separated us from a holy God, so now it separates us from an unholy world. Are we then walking apart from all which that world contains of vanity, or lust, or pleasure, or companionship, like men who have bidden them no unwilling adieu?

As those whose 'life is hid with Christ in God,' are we looking for his arrival, knowing that, 'when he who is our life shall appear, then shall we also appear with him in glory'? (Col. 3:4.) As those who have no city here, but, like

Abel or like Abraham, are content to be strangers on earth, are we expecting 'the city of habitations,' and anticipating the promise, 'Blessed are they that do his commandments, that they may have right to the tree of life [from which Adam was shut out], and may enter in through the gates into the city'? (Rev. 22:14.) And as those who are dwelling, for a while, outside of Eden, because of the first Adam's sin, are we holding fast our hope of entrance into the better Eden, of which we have been made the heirs, through the righteousness of the second Adam, who is the Lord from heaven?

Or, reader, is your life that of Cain—like those of whom it is written, 'Woe unto them! for they have gone in the way of Cain' (Jude 11)? His 'way' was 'according to the course of this world.' His portion was here. He built a city and dwelt in it, as one who was resolved to make the earth his home, and whose object was to be happy and prosperous without God. The life of the pilgrim did not suit his taste. A present home, not a future one, is what he seeks. It matters not to him though that home be in the land of the brier and the thorn. He prefers that to the hope of the incorruptible inheritance. This world is the vessel in which all his joys are freighted. Out of it, or beyond it, he has no hope. It is the treasure-house in which he has laid up his gold and silver.

Cain's world was one in which God was not; nay, in which it was impossible that God could be: for the friendship of that world was enmity with God, and friendship with God was enmity with that world. Thoughts of God would be unwelcome visitors, like drops of wormwood in the cup, or clouds drawn across the sun. Cain's object would be to multiply his occupations and enjoyments, so as to prevent God, and the things of God, from having any place in his soul. Thus would he try to steep his conscience in forgetfulness—forgetfulness of his sins, forgetfulness of God. Cares, burdens, toils, would be nought to him, if they could only assist him in shutting out God.

Cain's religion would be like all his other occupations, an instrument for keeping God at a distance and preventing Him from getting access to the soul. This is, perhaps, strange and almost incredible; yet we see it exemplified every day. What is the religion of most men? Is it a life of happy fellowship with God, the loving service of a gracious master? Nay, its object is to soothe or stifle an unquiet conscience, which is ever and anon witnessing for God, and for His claims, in the midst of the busiest scenes. It is performed as a sort of bribe, to induce God not to trouble them with His claims. Instead of being delighted in, as that which brings them into the presence of God and keeps them there, it is merely *submitted* to—and that for the purpose of excluding God altogether. They seem to go to their knees with this as the burden of their prayers, 'Depart from us.' This was Cain's religion. This is the world's religion still. Nay, it is *man's* religion. A world without God, and a religion framed for the purpose of shutting out God—these are the two things which man would fain secure for himself.

Is this your lot, reader? Has it long been so; and are you not most thoroughly weary of it? Or are you content that it should be so? Is this to be your heaven—your inheritance? And is it so desirable, that you find it worthwhile risking your eternity, to retain it for a few swift years? Perhaps you do think it a pleasant lot. But is it durable? And if it be not durable, is it wise to make it your all, so that when it fails you are without a hope? Would it not be well to look beyond it and see what may succeed? For if that which follows be eternal, is it not blind recklessness on your part, to make no provision for it? Before casting yourself headlong into the stream of present joy, have you taken security against the rising flood of unending sorrow? Can you either bribe or brave the judge? Are you prepared to do battle for life and joy, upon the shores of death and woe?

Is hell a fable, or the second death a picture of the fancy? That would indeed be good news to millions; for life's weariness would soon be over, and then all the past would lie behind them as a troubled dream. But who has come back from the grave to tell us this? Who has gone down into the depths of the earth, or visited each outlying star, or traversed the breadth of space; and then returned to us with these tidings on his lips, 'There is no hell'? Yet, even were hell a fiction, what becomes of *sin*? Is *it* to cease? If so, who is to dry up its stream, so that every drop shall evaporate? And if it ceases not, will there not be anguish enough to make a wretched eternity? Leave but the sinner to sin on forever, without a fetter to gall him, or a flame to scorch him, or a fiend to mock him, and he will wring his hands in agony, longing for annihilation, and wishing, a thousand times an hour, that he had never been born.

And if the second death be a fable, are the foretastes of it here but fables too? Is disease a fable, at which the wise man can smile? Is bodily anguish a fable, devised to 'overset the joys of life'? Is there no reality in tears, in partings, in bereavements, in broken hearts? Ah, if these present sorrows be no fiction, why delude ourselves with the fancy that these, or worse than these, cannot exist hereafter? Rather, are they not the foretastes of what shall be the everlasting portion of the ungodly? Are they not the shadows cast from the 'dark mountains' upon the plains of earth? And if the shadows be so sad and gloomy, what must that region itself be, from whose dark heights they fall?

Is heaven a dream? Surely, at least, it is a pleasant one— the dream of the happy! Whose dream, then, can it be? Can a child of sin and sadness here, dream so fair a dream? How came such images of the beautiful and the infinite into a soul so narrow, so defiled? Are the dreams of a poor mortal, brighter and more blessed than the realities of God? Whence come these 'immortal longings,' that seem like the reflected sunbeams of a purer firmament, towards which we are moving upwards?

Besides, who of men or angels has gone forth over space, even to its outermost circle, bringing back to us the heavy news, 'There is no heaven'? If there had, could we credit the tidings? Should we not say, 'Impossible! If there be a God, there must be a heaven; if there be here on earth that which we call fair, there must be somewhere else that which is fairer far; if there exist around us the beautiful and gladsome, must there not be a fountainhead of gladness and beauty'? For, do not the fair objects with which even this ruined earth is brightened, tell us that there must be, somewhere, a heaven? From them we get passing gleams of the beautiful and the perfect. Like stray particles of gold, they indicate the treasures of the mine beneath. Like lights gleaming from some palace window, they make known something of the splendour within. The various objects of sky and earth point to scenes of excellence and blessedness, of which they can only shadow forth the cold outline. The stars above us, as they give forth their never-ceasing radiance, unite in saying, 'There is a heaven—a heaven to which our brightness is as darkness itself.' The fields, the flowers, the streams of earth, all tell us 'there is a heaven—a lost paradise of which we are but the faded relics—a paradise yet to be inherited, of which we are the certain pledges.'

Heaven, then, is real; and, oh! what is that reality to be to you? Is that real heaven, that true blessedness, to be your portion forever? Or is the world to be your substitute for God? Is the wilderness to be your Eden, evil your good, and earth your only heaven? This cannot satisfy. These souls of yours are made for something more excellent and more enduring.

Refuse this heritage, and where shall you find another? God has but one heaven, and you treat it as a dream. Who can create one for you, or how shall you be able to do without one, when life, with its glow and dazzle, has faded away? And what shall become of your *capacity* for containing happiness—a boundless capacity, with which he who made you has endowed you? Can you shake it off, or lessen it, or make it content with the finite and the mortal? It is an appalling thought that there should be in you such a capacity as this! It is this—if one may speak after the manner of men, yet with reverence—it is this that gives God such a fearful, such an indissoluble hold of you. He can make you so blessed, and he can make you so wretched! That capacity for joy or sorrow, you cannot eradicate or alter. It exists in you, and must remain forever. That soul of yours is a vessel of amazing dimensions, and it cannot remain empty. It must be filled to the brim. Either joy or sorrow must be pouring into it throughout eternity. What a thought! Does it not startle you in your sins? Does it not force itself in upon your busiest and most mirthful hours, like a spectre from the realms of death?*

Can you know all this, and still remain heedless? Do you still cleave to the world as your friend—a world

---

*   Has not one of the world's own poets spoken out the world's feelings on this point, in language which men would do well to ponder?—

    'But ever and anon, for grief subdued,
    There comes a token like a serpent's sting;
    Scarce seen, but with fresh bitterness imbued;
    And slight withal may be the things which bring
    Back on the heart the weight which it would fling
    Aside forever. It may be a sound,
    A tone of music, summer's eve, or spring,
    A flower, the wind, the ocean, which shall sound,
    Striking the electric chain wherewith we're darkly bound.'—Byron

that knows not God, a world that is preparing for the devouring fire?

Think how much you lose. The forgiveness of sin, and the life everlasting—these you lose. The favour of God, the heirship of the kingdom, the lustre of an unfading crown—these you lose. The value of these is infinite, and the blessedness of possessing them is what you can neither measure nor conceive. The loss, which you are thus so deliberately incurring, is one for which there can be no equivalent, one which admits of no repair. The dark morning of your eternity is not one which will gradually brighten, till you find yourself once more in a circle of light and a land of hope. It is but the foretaste of 'the blackness of darkness forever.' You may fondly dream, as men do of the things of earth, that better days will come. You may vainly congratulate yourself, as the prince of the fallen is represented as doing—'this horror will grow mild, this darkness light.' But they never will. They are the inheritance which you have been preparing for yourself, the inheritance for which you have sold your immortal spirit, and it shall be yours forever. Once shut in within the walls of that region of fire and gloom, you shall go out no more.

And what is your gain? Your loss is infinite, is your gain any recompense? Alas! What do you gain? A little gold, a little mirth, a little vanity, perhaps a little fame and honour; that is all! And what do these amount to? A handful of withered leaves, which you may gather up in some autumn hollow! A dream of the beautiful, such as visits the cell of the prisoner only to cheat and mock him! This is all your gain on earth, and as for your gain hereafter, it is chains, and fire, and torment—the death that never dies, the 'second death,' to which no saviour comes, as 'the resurrection and the life.'

Yet why incur a loss so vast and so irretrievable, or why snatch at such wretched gain? Is there a necessity for this? Must you lose so much, and must you gain so little? It is not so. That gain and that loss are alike matters of your own deliberate and eager choice. That choice you have been making, not once, but a thousand times over. Often has God stepped in and expostulated with you, entreating you to reconsider the choice that you had made. But you refused to alter it. Often has he broken your idols, and emptied your storehouse, and withered your blossoms, in order that you might see the vanity of your choice. But you would not be taught. Often has some faithful friend or minister laid his hands upon yours, and remonstrated with you on the folly and the danger of your choice. But you would not listen. You persisted in following it out, and risking the consequences. You would not be turned out of the path which you were pursuing; you treated as rudeness the kind entreaties of friendship; you begged to be allowed to follow your own course, without the annoyance of such uncalled for and needless interference.

But still we interfere. We cannot see you go down to death unhindered and unbesought. We must again ask you to review your choice. Is it a wise one? Does it satisfy your own conscience? Have you not misgivings, not a few, respecting it? And if there be so much as one doubt in the matter, why persist in it?

Is there not a wiser, safer course? And do you not see the finger of God beckoning you to pursue it? Do you not hear his gracious voice announcing, 'As I live, saith the Lord God, I have no pleasure in the death of the wicked; but that the wicked turn from his way and live: turn ye, turn ye, from your evil ways; for why will ye die' (Ezek. 33:11)? Is not the God that made you, here pointing out a more excellent way? He speaks of life, and bids you take it freely. He speaks of death, and beseeches you to avoid it. He asks you to return to him who still yearns over you, and waits to show his grace.

It is thus that a writer of the olden time sets himself to plead with such as you:

> Never did Jacob with such joy weep over the neck of his Joseph as thy heavenly Father would rejoice over thee upon thy coming in to him. Look over the story of the prodigal. Methinks I see how the aged father lays aside his state, and forgetteth his years. Behold how he runneth! Oh, the haste that mercy makes! The sinner makes not half that speed. Methinks I see how his bowels turn, how his compassions yearn. How quick sighted is love! Mercy spies him a great way off, forgets his riotous courses, unnatural rebellion, horrid unthankfulness (not a word of these), receives him with open arms, clasps his neck, forgets his rags, kisses his lips, calls for the fatted calf, the best robe, the ring, the shoes, the best cheer in heaven's store, the best attire in heaven's wardrobe. Yea, the joy

cannot be held in one breast. Others must be called in to share. The friends must meet and make merry. Angels must wait, but the prodigal must sit at table, under his father's wing. He is the joy of the feast, the object of the father's delight. The friends sympathise, but none knows the felicity the father takes in his newborn son, whom he hath received from the dead. Methinks I hear the music and the dancing at a distance! Oh, the melody of the heavenly choristers! I cannot learn the song, but methinks I overhear the burden, at which all the harmonious choir, with one consent, strike sweetly in, for this goes round at heaven's table, "This my son was dead, and is alive again; he was lost, and is found."*

It is no toilsome pilgrimage on which He asks you to set out, in order to reach His dwelling. He Himself has come to you, nay, sits by your very side, as did Jesus by the side of the woman of Sychar. He does not bid you climb to heaven, in order to find grace there. Neither does he tell you to go down into the deep, in order to obtain it there. He has opened the fountain at your very side. He takes up the vessel and presses it to your lips. 'The word is nigh thee, even in thy mouth and in thy heart, that is, the word of life which we preach, that if thou shalt confess with thy mouth the Lord Jesus, and shalt believe in thine heart that God hath raised him from the dead, *thou shalt be saved*' (Rom. 10:8-9).

To you, lover of pleasure, dreamer of earth's dreams, God is telling, this day, the story of His free love, that,

---

*   Alleine's *Alarm to the Unconverted.*

receiving it, you may not perish, but have everlasting life. That free love thus received into your heart in *believing*, would fill you with joy unspeakable. It would be like fragrance from the flowers of Eden, like sunshine from the very heaven of heavens. It would be better to you than pleasure, or gold, or lust; better than all the joys of earth poured into one jewelled cup. It would demand no price of you, neither would it call on you to wait till you had made yourself ready for receiving it. It would come into you at once, like sunlight into your lattice, without insisting that your chamber be adorned for its reception. It would cost you nothing, but the giving up of that which is far better lost, and the gain of which would be a poor recompense for a ruined soul and an eternity of hopeless sorrow.

THE END.

For more Horatius and Andrew Bonar books available from
Christian Focus Publications

visit christianfocus.com

God's Way of Holiness
Growing in Grace by Walking with God
Horatius Bonar

978-1-5271-0610-9

Horatius Bonar shows us that a life that has been saved is a life that is holy. The Spirit of God works in us to make us holy. The saving work of Christ on the cross has given us the victory over sin, but while we are on this earth we battle on. Read and be encouraged.

God's Way of Peace

Overcoming Anxiety by Walking with God

Horatius Bonar

978-1-5271-0609-3

This book for those who are anxious gently directs our eyes back to Jesus. Taking the whole message of the gospel, Horatius Bonar shows us that although we cannot save ourselves by our character or our works, we can have peace in the finished work of Jesus Christ.

The Person of Christ

Finding Assurance by Walking with Jesus

Andrew Bonar

978-1-5271-0971-1

A wonderful encouragement for Christians today. Despite the difference between this edition's original publication date, the truths Bonar addresses are timeless. Bonar sets out a precedent for heartfelt evangelical exposition of the Gospel via the personal relationship Christians have with the Person of Christ.

Christian Focus Publications

Our mission statement

Staying Faithful

In dependence upon God we seek to impact the world through literature faithful to His infallible Word, the Bible. Our aim is to ensure that the Lord Jesus Christ is presented as the only hope to obtain forgiveness of sin, live a useful life and look forward to heaven with Him.

Our Books are published in four imprints:

CHRISTIAN FOCUS

Popular works including biographies, commentaries, basic doctrine and Christian living.

MENTOR

Books written at a level suitable for Bible College and seminary students, pastors, and other serious readers. The imprint includes commentaries, doctrinal studies, examination of current issues and church history.

CHRISTIAN HERITAGE

Books representing some of the best material from the rich heritage of the church.

CF4KIDS

Children's books for quality Bible teaching and for all age groups: Sunday school curriculum, puzzle and activity books; personal and family devotional titles, biographies and inspirational stories – because you are never too young to know Jesus!

Christian Focus Publications Ltd,
Geanies House, Fearn, Ross-shire,
IV20 1TW, Scotland, United Kingdom.
www.christianfocus.com